D1132826

NEW YORK CITY'S

BEST DIVE BARS

NEW YORK CITY'S

BEST DIVE BARS

Drinking and Diving in the Big Apple

BEN WESTHOFF

Brooklyn, New York

Copyright © 2010 by Ben Westhoff
Photographs © 2010 by Ben Westhoff
All rights reserved.

Printed in the USA
10 9 8 7 6 5 4 3 2 1

No part of this book may be used or reproduced in any manner without written permission of the publisher. Please direct inquires to:

Gamble Guides is an imprint of
Ig Publishing
392 Clinton Avenue
Brooklyn, NY 11238
www.igpub.com

Author photo by Anna Westhoff

ACKNOWLEDGEMENTS

For Anna, Mom, Dad, Alex and Julia. Also, thanks to Dive Bar Ben and everyone else who journeyed with me to these remarkable, and remarkable-smelling, dives.

New York City's Best Dive Bars
(arranged by neighborhood)

What is a dive?

On one hand, many bar owners resent the word "dive" as they don't think it could possibly apply to *their* watering hole. Dives, they believe, are money-losing, decaying spots which cater to nasty old drunks. On the other hand, for young tipplers, the "dive" descriptor invokes images of a boozy Eden, gritty but pure, a place with cheap beer on every tap and whimsy around every corner. They imagine the regulars to be street-savvy gurus who, for what they lack in good looks and fancy clothes, make up for it in earnest, grizzled *realness*.

Both perceptions are hogwash. First off, plenty of dive bars make money—how else do you think they stay in business for fifty, sixty years? And their drunks aren't any wiser than the kind who drink at home or in more upscale bars. As a matter of fact, dive bar regulars don't usually consider their preferred pubs to be "dives," and the spots given that description by the young and privileged are usually too fancy to merit it.

So what is a dive then? A place with cheap drinks? Certainly not always in Manhattan. A dusty, dingy hole? Well, some of the best dives are spotlessly clean. An aging relic? Often, although many newish hipster bars have done a great job at capturing the dive aesthetic.

Ultimately, I had to come up with my own working definition, something more substantial than "you know it when you see it." (Although, you do. Look for Christmas lights.) A dive, I decided, has a stillness about it, an air that it is not driven by commerce, even if it ultimately is. It's a place where nobody tries to "upsell" you, where temporary solutions—say, duct tape over broken urinals—become permanent. A dive embraces your inner degenerate, doesn't judge, and doesn't pretend that drinking isn't the main task at hand.

Something else to keep in mind: Anyone who says that gentrified New York has no more dives is bonkers. Sure, we no longer have

McGurk's Suicide Hall, the Bowery haunt frequented by sailors and low-rent prostitutes that was thought to be *the place* to take one's own life. But we've still got the historic rooms, the cultural diversity and the unquenchable thirst that makes New York a great dive bar town. In fact, there were too many great dives for this book, as New York City has literally thousands of dive bars. Unfortunately, I couldn't go to all of them, so I focused on spots people buying this book would likely visit, mostly in lower Manhattan and the trendy Brooklyn neighborhoods. That said, the truly mind-boggling spots I've profiled tend to be above 100th Street or in the less glamorous boroughs. (If you're ever on Staten Island head immediately to Beer Goggles.)

So, enjoy these watering holes, and don't be afraid. While they aren't filled with intoxicated sages, they're not unwelcoming either. If a spot looks intimidating, just remember that your money is always welcome, and that liquor makes for strange barfellows.

Dive Bar Ratings

All bars are rated on a scale of one to five beer bottles, with five bottles denoting the diviest.

 Pleasantville

 Sin City

 Mean Streets

 The Warriors

 Apocalypse Now

TELLTALE SIGNS YOU'RE IN A DIVE BAR

- It looks closed, but it's open

- Christmas lights

- The women's room has a sign that says, "Ladies Only!"

- Upright, chrome cash registers

- Witty signs like: "Free Beer! Tomorrow"

- Wood-grain linoleum

- Tonic and other mixers dispensed via individual bottles

- When you pay for a five buck drink with a ten, you're given a five as a change instead of five ones. (This shows they're not scheming for a tip.)

- Red lighting and red vinyl booths

- Poor drink selection

- You're IDed not because you look young, but because you don't belong

- Multiple TVs on different channels, each with the sound on

- People making (and taking) calls on pay phones

NYC'S TEN BEST DIVES

(in no particular order)

O'Connor's Bar

Dublin House

Jimmy's Corner

Nancy Whiskey Pub

Blarney Cove

Holland Bar

Holiday Cocktail Lounge

Tip Top Bar & Grill

Alibi

Sunny's Bar

NEW YORK CITY'S BEST DIVE BARS

(IN ALPHABETICAL ORDER)

Freddy's Bar, R.I.P.

119 Bar

119 E 15th Street (Irving Place & E Union Square)
Transit: 4, 5, 6, L, N, Q, R, W to Union Square   *(212) 995-5904*

Tucker Max says he hopes they serve beer in hell. Well, they do. The only problem is that they serve it at Dave & Busters, which means that the suds are overpriced and you're surrounded by screaming video games. Heaven, however, is full of dives. Though their patrons aren't much to look at and the televisions aren't high definition, nobody cares. They had their entire earthly lives to stare at screens and lust after people they'd never be able to sleep with, so they come to dives for someone to talk to.

119 Bar has taken that minimalist aesthetic to its logical conclusion. There's virtually nothing to do here besides drink, play pool, talk and eat Zapp's BBQ potato chips. The walls are barren save for a poster of Frank Sinatra's mug shot, and the TV above the bar is left off, save for Mets and Giants games. "People get too distracted by television," the bartender told me. "They tend to just stare at it."

Though it is dark and the windows are obscured by thick curtains, 119 is a clean establishment: the tables are wiped, the floor swept. And while the seats and Chaise lounge may have foam showing, and the tables may feature graffiti on top of other graffiti, it's still a very sanitary type of disorder.

As in heaven, 119 Bar treats you to random, arbitrary discounts. When I ordered a pair of Jack and ginger ales the bartender had a moment of contemplation. "It would normally be $12," he said, "but we'll just say 10."

Dive Bar Rating 🍾🍾

169 Bar

169 East Broadway (Rutgers Street)
Transit: F to East Broadway

169barnyc.com
(212) 473-8866

A woman sitting at the bar was ignoring the complimentary peanuts in front of her, in favor of her own plastic bag of cashews. Black, mustachioed, and flirting with the halter-topped barkeep, she was serious about her liquor, evidenced by the fact that she was drinking from two glasses simultaneously.

Most 169 Bar denizens fit this description. (The part about being serious about their liquor, not the part about being hirsute females.) With its leopard-skin pool table, Chinese lanterns, red vinyl booths and palm fronds nestled in bottles of Patron, the place offers a terrific environment to be off your rocker.

The David Lynchian vibe is almost enough to make you forget that they filmed an episode of *Flight of the Conchords* here. After all, Bret and Jemaine's music would have a hard time finding its way onto the speakers at this eighty year-old Chinatown haunt, as owner/ musical curator Charles Hanson tends towards big band, jazz, blues and funk when there isn't a DJ or live rock band. The stage is right next to the front door, so you're forced to listen to the music no matter how bad it sucks. Thankfully, each act plays only thirty minute sets, and there's substantial down time between groups.

If you're interested in performing here, keep in mind that Hanson, a former New Orleans punk player who took over the place in 2006, has redecorated and reorganized the booking process, and there are tons of rules for bands nowadays; they must use the house drum kit, bring in a certain amount of customers, etc. After sets, the musicians become part of the crowd and begin eating their own cashews, grooming their own mustaches, or whatever.

Dive Bar Rating

2A

25 Avenue A (at East 2nd Street)
Transit: F, M to 2nd Ave-Houston   *(212) 505-2466*

2A is about as fancy as a bar can be and still qualify for this book. Still, its relative swank gets a pass because, as far as I know, it's the only place in Manhattan where a poorly-dressed Pabst drinker can enjoy second-floor views through floor to ceiling windows.

The ground level is nice too, and full of its own sharp architectural touches, like the wall of stacked glass cubes and the trap door behind the bar that leads down to the basement. But it's upstairs where you'll feel like you're living the good life. Benches butt up to the windows, which look out over the intersection of 2nd Street and Avenue A. You can get drinks up there as well, and the bartender's station has a beautifully-crafted wooden bar. Printed tin plates run along the bottoms of the walls, and much of the seating is comprised of plush, curved booths. These details will make you wonder how you're managing to drink cheaply here.

The bouncer is of the introspective variety, looking up from his mobile device not to see your ID, but to ask how you're doing tonight. He'll then wave you through if he deems it appropriate, and wish you well. If you're with someone you shouldn't be, go ahead and seat yourself in the almost-pitch black back corner of the first floor. Preferably, however, go upstairs and take in the views. It's kind of like one of those restaurants on the top floors of hotels, except for cheap guys who want to impress their dates.

Dive Bar Rating

Alibi

242 Dekalb Ave (Clermont Ave and Vanderbilt Ave)

Transit: G to Clinton-Washington; C toLafayette Ave   *(718) 783-8519*

Normally, I took notes for this book by sending myself text messages, as I stopped using pen and paper after the bartender/lap dancer at Navy Yard Cocktail Lounge ripped my notebook out of my hands and began reading my assessment of her dump aloud.

However, at Alibi I sort of lost my head. I'd heard that the venerable Fort Greene garden-level watering hole was a writer's hangout, and therefore I didn't think anyone would give me grief for jotting down notes in my Mead. And they probably wouldn't have, either, if I hadn't done it while peeing. "That's what I call multitasking!" chided the gaunt guy with the cigarette behind his ear at the urinal next to me. He then proceeded to compare me to women who drive while applying make-up. "In America, we've got to cut that shit out!" he concluded. Walking out of the rest room, he proceeded to flirt with my friend Anna—a different Anna than my wife Anna, but still—and then, to top it all off, he bounced the cue ball off of a bumper and sent it directly into the corner pocket on the other side of the pool table. Damn.

But who cares? Alibi is the perfect dive bar, equally grungy and comfy. "It seems kinda borderline welcoming, almost," said Anna's husband Justin, nailing it. The tin ceiling hangs low, the fireplace props up 8 Ball trophies and is full of debris, and the unvarnished wooden tables have an eighth-grade girls' school worth of gum under them. The bartender calls the Brooklyn Lager simply "Lager," like they do with Yuengling in Philly; that might be because there's not much else by way of selection. They've got a dozen bottles of Jameson behind the bar and seemingly little else, but my happy-hour serving of said Irish whiskey was only $3, so there's that. And Anna's Coke was free.

In conclusion, yes, Alibi is a writer's bar, but don't get cocky.

Dive Bar Rating 🍾🍾🍾🍾

Antarctica

287 Hudson Street (Dominick Str and Spring St)

Transit: C, E to Spring St; 1 to Houston   *(212) 352-1666*

Great gimmicks birth great bars, and Antarctica's got a doozy: Each day a staffer writes down a random first name on the front board, and anyone who walks in with that name drinks free that night. Simple and pretty brilliant, although it requires some enforcement. "We absolutely demand I.D.," the genial redheaded barkeep told me. "People try to scam me every day."

Does she allow for spelling variations? For example, the day I was there the posted name was "Phillip." Would "Philip" be okay? "It would depend on his attitude and the size of his group," she went on. "If he brought a large, paying, posse I'd let it slide." Most importantly, she didn't have to add, remember that "free" does not include gratuity. "Real winners tip!" reads the board.

Even if you're not named Phillip, or Elsa or Helena or Marley or Ishan or any of the other fairly-obscure winning monikers that pop up there, Antarctica is a low-key, spacious place to kick it between Canal and Houston. It's the antithesis of nearby Nancy Whiskey Pub, which is crowded, inexpensive, intense and full of weirdos. At Antarctica, a Corona will cost you $6.50, but in return you get an airy, scrubbed facility to lounge in, one with exposed brick and pretty wood plank floors.

The place is considered something of a haven for pool players, if only because it provides sufficient elbow room to actually get off a shot. The extensive house rules state, in part: "Skip shots okay;" "Spotting 8-Ball after scratch okay;" "Peace, love and understanding." I have no idea what any of that means, but the assembled sharks do. When I was there they were gay and had brought cues from home, carrying them inside leather cases that looked designed to hold shotguns. I've got a sneaking suspicion at least one of them was named Phillip.

Dive Bar Rating

B Side

204 Avenue B (12th & 13th Sts.)

Transit: L to 1st Ave   *(212) 475-4600*

Some people call B Side a punk dive, but I find it to be more of a dyke dive. There's red mood lighting, pin-up girls painted on metal canvases, and a steel bar. There's also a bartender with a shark fin hairdo, who was staring at my wife Anna when we were there. Another of the bartenders, Amy, sells her own brand of trail mix on the premises. It's called "Best Snack Ever," and the original variation features candied pecans, pistachios, roasted and seasoned walnuts, dark chocolate covered raisins, and peanut butter chips. A cut above your average GORP, for sure.

Despite the ovarian vibe, the place is ballsy. They either don't have air-conditioning or else opt not to run it, perhaps for the thrill of seeing people sweat. The music tends toward slowcore when it's not punk, and their most popular drink special is a can of PBR and a shot of well whisky for $5. That's the quintessential New York dive bar special, actually, and it says a lot about a place—namely that it's not sponsored by any big liquor companies and its clientele is not snobbish about what it dumps down its gullet.

Unlike some dives, B Side is not crawling with grizzled, thickly-bearded, toothless men. There was only one person like that when we were there, and he was bragging about having scored a free pint from an anonymous stranger bragging that "he didn't trust anyone who didn't drink."

A sweaty room full of mostly women drinking cheap booze and eating GORP, that's pretty much B Side in a nutshell. There are worse places to spend your time.

Dive Bar Rating

Barrow's Pub

463 Hudson Street (Barrow St and Morton St)

Transit: 1 to Houston St; A, C, E, B, D, F, M to W 4th   *(212) 741-9349*

Is there anything more inspiring than a shrinking old man flirting his ass off? The resident google-genarian at Barrow's Pub sports one of those caps that snap in the front—the kind Jeff Tweedy used to wear—and a shirt that says, "You Know You're Getting Old When Happy Hour Is A Nap." He drinks Bud from a brandy glass and plays that lottery game involving grids of numbers on the television. Both are mainly excuses to chat up the freckled, blonde bartender.

Still, Barrow's is no old man bar. The music see-saws from Jamie Foxx to Fleetwood Mac to Modest Mouse, and the night I was there the place was full of late twenty-something and early thirty-something women in mini-dresses. They came in a rush with their gay male friends and a pizza. (Barrow's sells pies itself, for six dollars, but no one seemed to care.) To the tune of Tina Turner's "Private Dancer," a light-skinned crew member gyrated, strip-tease style, for one of the guys. Quoth the codger: "The dancing girls are here!"

A pint of Grolsch is $6.50, and PBR is a little cheaper. (It's the West Village—what can you do?) In any case, Barrow's is surely the diviest spot in the neighborhood, much divier than Johnny's Bar or Julius. It's got quirks galore, like the secret wooden panels that reveal the air-conditioning controls and the sign that says "Finish your beer, there's sober kids in India." The TV showing the Yankees game is almost impossible to see because it's blocked by the pool lights, and the words "We Now Carry Mich Ultra" take up the entire mirror behind the bar. Big news, indeed.

Dive Bar Rating

MOST TERRIFYING DIVES

Navy Yard Cocktail Lounge

Beer Goggles

Cordato's Deli and Bar

Crehan's Pub

Station Cafe

Holland Bar

Beer Goggles Bar & Grill

293 Van Duzer Street

Transit: Stapleton [Staten Island Railway] *(718) 816-4537*

Beer Goggles Bar & Grill allegedly hires unlicensed bouncers, its owner has been charged with operating as a bookie, and the place has been raided by police who took sledgehammers to illegal gambling machines. (Perhaps unaware they were being caught on video, the cops proceeded to stuff the cash into their pockets.) But the bar is perhaps best known for a 2008 incident in which a pair of policemen caught the bartenders serving minors. The uniformed officers proceeded to hand out summonses and order the place shut down. The pub's denizens didn't take this lying down, however, as s pair of drunk barflies attacked the cops, sending one of them to the hospital. It turned out that the assailants were off-duty firemen, which stoked a new wave of animosity between the NYPD and the FDNY. (Resentment still lingers between the groups, dating back to 9/11 when Giuliani scaled back the Fire Department's recovery role and a bunch of firefighters went bananas, knocking over barricades and throwing blows at police.) The aftermath of Staten Island's "Battle of the Badges"? The policeman had emergency surgery on his hand and the firefighters were suspended without pay for a month. Beer Goggles, however, was back open within a week.

With its perfect combination of seediness, depravity and creature comforts, it's not hard to see why people would risk their lives for the place. First of all, it's well-named. The "the more I drink, the better you look" theme is highlighted by a psychedelic, black-lit mural that features the bar's bespectacled Clark Kent-esque mascot holding up a frothy mug and noting its ability to "Turn BOW into WOW!" In that same room is the best air hockey machine I've ever played on, a neon green unit that makes a cool metallic sound whenever the puck hits the side bumpers. There's also a vending machine selling cigarettes and a "male enhancement" pill called VIM-25. (Read: a Viagra-substitute composed of Chinese herbs.) The drinks are cheap, too. At least I think they are. After my buddy Brandon and I ordered a couple of beers the bartender—a fairly slow, rather slovenly, guy—told us they would be ten dollars. We gave him a twenty and he handed back our change, which came to exactly fifteen dollars.

Brandon, a touring musician who recently moved onto the island, insists that the right-leaning, architecturally-challenged borough has its own culture, one as far removed from Manhattan as it is from Cleveland. To him, this isn't a good thing. But hell, he lives cheaply, has ample parking for his van and, if nothing else, goes to sleep knowing his firemen will fight to keep the local dive bars open.

Dive Bar Rating

Billymark's West

332 9th Avenue, (29th Street & 30th Street)
Transit: A,C,E to 34th St, 1,2,3 to 34th St

(212) 629-0118

Shortly after my friend Jeff and I arrived at Billymark's West, co-owner and bartender Billy Penza cranked up The Weather Girls, singing along to "It's Raining Men." Dressed in a short-sleeved shirt the color of Fruit Stripe gum and wearing thick black glasses, he proceeded to guzzle a glass of ale and light up a cigarette before scurrying outside. When he returned a little while later, he told us about the framed platinum albums behind the bar, which belong to his brother Mark, who is the establishment's other owner (Billy—Mark, get it?) and a former session drummer for Blondie.

Later on in the evening, Billy offered up a very honest assessment of the beverages available at the bar. Blue Moon is "delicious," while a grenade-shaped energy drink called Bomba is, "terrible. Do not try it." All along, he wasn't writing down what we had been ordering, instead tallying everything in his head, which was not a very accurate system; when the bill came due at the conclusion of the evening, he ended up undercharging us. We found this to be fair enough, however, as the prices here are a tad on the high side.

The good news is that the energy level is similarly elevated. The plastic-paneled jukebox belts out disco songs like Jeff Redd's "Keep Dancing," which you might want to look up. People keep score during their dart games by writing directly on the aqua-colored walls in chalk. The clientele runs from servicemen to softball players to mailmen. The postal servant sitting next to me, armed with a shot, mixed drink and beer, told me that I couldn't leave until the bottles behind the bar were empty. While it may sound like a silly thing to say, it's actually a drunkard's platonic ideal: Imagine a bender so epic it leaves the bar utterly extinguished, every drink drunk dry.

Dive Bar Rating

OTHERWORLDLY FEEL

Puerto Rico USA Bar

Mars Bar

Nancy Whiskey Pub

Irene's Pub

Beer Goggles

Port 41

Desmond's Tavern

Mr. McGoo's

Blarney Cove

510 E 14th Street (Avenue A & Avenue B)

Transit: L to 1st Ave

(212) 473-9284

Moments after I took that picture of the Blarney Cove, a woman came running out of the place.

"Why are you taking pictures of my bar?" she asked, half-crazed. She was middle-aged and had lipstick all over her teeth. I explained that I was writing a book. She demanded my name and phone number, in case she had any "questions" for me. Kind of scared, I wrote both down. She asked when she could call, and I said, um, any time so long as it was during normal hours. She asked what I meant by "normal." Then she gestured at the slice of pizza I was holding. "Give me some," she demanded. She ate nearly half of what was left before telling me it wasn't very good, and that I should have gone to Artichoke instead. She said her name was Margie. I then went to meet up with some friends at Otto's Shrunken Head. Later on, we went back to Blarney Cove and sat down at the bar. However, Margie didn't notice me come in, as she was too busy drinking and head-banging to the Beastie Boys, offering up her own altered lyrics: *You've gotta fight/ For your right/ For beer!*

Blarney Cove is the real deal, a long sliver with one wood-paneled wall and one faux-bricked wall. It's the kind of place where a guy wearing a straw fedora will smoke a cigarette while playing video poker and then mash the butt on the floor with his shoe once he's done. The type of spot with a pay phone where people regularly receive calls and a gumball machine that dispenses pistachios.

Eventually, Margie recognized me, coming over, grabbing my hand tightly and pulling me to the other side of the bar. She introduced me to a guy with a thin mustache, a photographer, and a beefy guy called "Popeye." According to commenters on Yelp, Popeye is former NYPD and kind of an asshole.

"Next time you must ask Popeye before you take pictures. He's in charge."

"I thought it was your bar?"

"Popeye's in charge."

In truth, nobody's in charge at Blarney Cove. It has its own forward momentum, slowly spiraling out of control.

Dive Bar Rating

Blue & Gold Tavern

79 E. 7th Street (1st Ave and 2nd Ave)

Transit: 6 to Astor Place; L to 1st Ave; F to 2nd Ave　　*(212) 473-8918*

Mike, the bartender at the Blue & Gold Tavern, keeps the top couple of buttons on his shirt undone, which shows off his thick chest hair. He also keeps his shirtsleeves rolled up and drinks thirstily from a gallon jug of Poland Spring water. Mike does all of this even when it's cold outside because he's always warm, keeping himself busy lining up glassware on the shelves behind the bar and dishing out the tavern's history.

The place was opened on March 19, 1958 by his grandfather, also named Mike. "He was named after me," Mike jokes, adding that he prefers not to give out their last name. Granddad came to the U.S. after World War II, from the Ukraine. (Blue & Gold's name is assumedly a reference to the colors of that country's flag.)

Mike doesn't mind if you call his family's establishment a dive, and takes particular pride in its low prices. Vazac's Horseshoe Bar is not a real dive, he contends, because it's too expensive. Indeed, booze is absurdly cheap here; $3 for drinks made with (or shots of) Jim Beam, $3.50 for Jack Daniels, and $4 for Macallan, or "The Macallan," as the single malt scotch calls itself. The atmosphere is cozy, with Christmas wreaths still hanging long after the holiday has ended. Most tables double as chess, backgammon or Scrabble boards, although the Scrabble table is too mucked up to permit a full game. The music is kept low, which is nice if your tastes don't jibe with that of those who dominate the place, mainly kids who are closer to twenty than thirty.

In any case, here's to the Blue & Gold. May its metaphorical flag continue to fly, may its drink prices stay the same.

Dive Bar Rating

The Blue Donkey Bar

489 Amsterdam Aven (83rd and 84th Streets)

212-496-0777   *Transit: 1 to 86th St; B,C to 81st St*

Opening a bar next door to your greasy spoon is an idea so brilliant it's a wonder more people don't do it. Connecting the two establishments at the back and filling them with arcade games? That's downright inspired.

The Blue Donkey Bar and its adjacent sister restaurant Homer's Blue Donkey Grill combine to form something of a pleasure factory for kids and adults. Both places sell drinks and feature games; the Grill has Ms. Pac Man and one of those Japanese "Drift" style racers, the Bar has Big Buck Safari, pool and foosball. The Grill will make you sliders, curly fries and milk shakes until late most nights, while the Bar features keeps in barely-there mini-dresses.

The Blue Donkey Bar is perhaps the quintessential Upper West Side dive, possessing a retro-futuristic, space-age interior with a glowing orb and illuminated blue panel above the bar. The inhabiting cast of characters are a bit otherwordly, too: graying, well-composed whisky imbibers, prostitutes flirting with hairy Hawaiian guys and lazy entrepreneurs drinking Bud at the bar while hawking pirated DVDs. Also present are slightly-too-ironic-for-the-neighborhood twenty and thirtysomethings who come for the cheap quart bottles of Sol and the twenty-four ounce cans of Natty Light and Colt 45. Those who are slightly more discriminating can get a bottle of Jimmy Buffet's Corona-like Land Shark beer, or at the very least knock around some of that brand's promotional beach balls hanging from the ceiling. The best thing to do, however, is to act like you're at a Chuck E. Cheese. Blitz yourself on sugar, fat and alcohol and spend your quarters recklessly. A night at the Blue Donkey necessitates sacrificing your body to many forms of indulgence.

Dive Bar Rating

BEST HIPSTER DIVES

(in no particular order)

Hank's Saloon

Parkside Lounge

119 Bar

Bushwick Country Club

Turkey's Nest Tavern

Doc Holliday's

Welcome To The Johnson's

Bohemian Hall & Beer Garden

2919 24th Avenue, at 29th Street　　　　*www.bohemianhall.com*

Transit: N, W to Astoria Blvd.　　　　　*(718) 274-4925*

The Bohemian Hall & Beer Garden looks like a prison from the outside, but inside lurks the most fun a Czech can have in New York City (or Astoria, to be more precise). Ringed by tall stone walls, this palatial beer garden offers European beers to go along with beef stroganoff, beef goulash and perogies, as well as just about every other combination of onions, milk, potatoes and cow you can imagine.

Upon entry to the hall, you'll first encounter the spartanly-furnished bar, which may have folk music playing and basketball or boxing on the TV. Further in is the dining area, which, chockablock with light-colored tables and chairs, looks like the showroom for an unpainted furniture warehouse. But the real action is outside, where, when the weather's good, hundreds of young Queens go-getters lurk, likely attractive and probably sauced. Ladies sport oversized white sunglasses, guys smoke cigarettes and wear designer tennies, and everyone sits at picnic tables atop concrete and gravel, drinking large mugs of imported lagers, pilsners and hefeweizens. It's a typical beer garden—not fancy, but familial. At the center sits a large bandstand where, if you're lucky, you'll see performances by folks outfitted in traditional Bohemian garb. Think bonnets and bodices.

The building's upstairs houses a Czech and Slovak school, not to mention a full-on dance floor complete with disco ball. (If you play your cards right, you might get the opportunity to learn some folk steps from resident children's dance group Limborá ek-Limborá ik.) The space also offers an entertainment schedule sure to please Czech nationals and outer borough indie-rockers alike, including jazz shows, ping pong tournaments, low budget films and one-man plays.

Run by the Bohemian Citizens' Benevolent Society of Astoria, Bohemian Hall is a hundred years old, and bills itself as the "last original remaining Beer Garden" in the city. Consider it your role as amateur international goodwill ambassador, then, to order up an extra Hoegaarden.

Dive Bar Rating

Botanica

47 E. Houston Street (Greene Street & Mott Street)

Transit: 6, B, D, F, M to Broadway-Lafayette   *(212) 343-7251*

When the young folks at Milano's Bar are scared off by the middle-aged drunks, they head over to Botanica, just a few yards away. As opposed to the old New York flavor of Milano's, Botanica is decorated like the owners went on a shopping spree at a Midwestern garage sale. You've never seen such an assortment of rickety Formica tables, lamps made from booze bottles, mirrors that look like they belong on a pirate ship and Chinese lanterns. The atmosphere is reminiscent of 169 Bar, minus the noir element.

In the back there's an isolated room that theoretically offers a bit of privacy when it's slow, although when I go it's usually full of twenty-something girls cackling hysterically. Up front the bartender is prematurely balding and usually wearing an orange cardigan sweater. He serves up drinks like an $8 wasabi martini and something that requires minced ginger, which he carefully spoons out of a jar.

If you like fancy drinks coupled with grungy décor, this is your place. The bathrooms are not only unmarked, but they lack door handles as well. A piece of graffiti inside one reads, "Faux-tanica!" but that's a bit unfair. Botanica might not be the diviest dive around, but its hipsters are spirited, its floors are sloped, and its furniture seems to come directly from Muncie, Indiana. If you're a baby boomer you belong at Milano's, but if you're young and you're not having a good time at Botanica, then you should probably have another drink.

Dive Bar Rating

UNLIKELY TO HAVE HIPSTERS

Irene's Pub

Puerto Rico USA Bar

Holland Bar

Irish Eyes

Desmond's Tavern

Homestretch Pub

Joe's Bar & Grill

Crehan's Pub

Station Cafe

Brooklyn Ice House

318 Van Brunt St (Pioneer St and King St)

Transit: Cab it from Carroll Street subway stop (F)   *(718) 222-1865*

If it's true, per rumor, that the Brooklyn Ice House and the dive bar sitting right next to it, Red Hook Bait & Tackle, send each other their drunks when they get out of hand, then Red Hook Bait & Tackle surely gets the short end of the stick, as you'll generally find an artier crowd there than the hard-poundin', hard eatin' lot that populate the Ice House, although the latter's folks are not necessarily unsophisticated.

Formerly known as Pioneer Bar-B-Q, the place serves up beef brisket and pulled pork sandwiches, and is also known for its cheap shots—$3, all the time—and its potty mouth humor. (Sign in the front window: "Have you pulled your pork today?") But what struck me is how the Ice House somehow perfectly walks a line between highbrow and lowbrow. For every un-tethered dog licking your ankles and gap-toothed fat guy grinning creepily, there's a dude typing on his laptop and a $7 Belgian beer on tap. (Try the La Chouffe. It's good, kind of an herbal taste. My wife told me that.)

They've also got a *Family Guy* pinball machine (lowbrow) and board games including Candy Land (highbrow), Boggle (highbrow) and Pop Smarts (lowbrow). Your ass will feel every single spring in the vinyl booth running along the side of the wall, but you won't notice it, so busy will you be trying to figure out what music is playing overhead. It's the *Miami Vice* theme song, you'll finally realize, but as to whether that's highbrow or lowbrow, it's impossible to say.

Dive Bar Rating

NEW YORK CITY'S BEST DIVE BARS

Bushwick Country Club

618 Grand St (Leonard St & Lorimer St)   *www.bushwickcountryclub.com*

Transit: G,L to Metropolitan Ave-Lorimer St   *(718) 388-2114*

WILLIAMSBURG, BROOKLYN

As is often noted, Bushwick Country Club is not in Bushwick and it is not a country club. Located on the southeastern outskirts of Williamsburg, the bar is named after *Caddyshack's* Bushwood Country Club, and boasts six holes of mini golf in its back yard. Ask the bartender for putters—no charge, he'll just want an ID—and knock yourself out. The tiny course is highlighted by a windmill made out of PBR cans but is otherwise sparsely-decorated. (The bar recently ran a contest for people to design their own hole, with the winner to receive a $100 bar tab and a plaque with his or her name on it.)

Micro-duffing aside, Bushwick Country Club is the near perfect hipster dive bar, featuring a photo booth, Big Buck Hunter, Safari edition, gratis cheesy puffs and comely, tastefully tattooed young ladies who stalk the premises in packs. My only complaint is the alcoholic slushies. The $6 cherry and vodka concoction—poured directly from a machine—is a high-fructose corn syrup nightmare. Before half of my mug was done I was bouncing off the walls, only to experience a sugar crash moments later. I asked the mustachioed bartender for some help, and he filled the rest of the mug with ice and vodka for five more dollars, but this did little to dilute the cough syrup flavor. A drunken/ slightly-deranged/ oddly-articulate barfly named Andy insisted that five cheesy puffs would sufficiently wash the cherry taste out of my mouth. ("I just grew another point in my crown!" he enthused after giving me this advice.) For what it's worth, I'm told the Jim Beam and Coke slushie is more manageable (once in a while they have Makers Mark milkshakes.)

Ask at the bar about becoming a "member" of Bushwick Country Club, which entitles you to drink specials and other perks. Throw a party on your birthday and bring in 15 people (11 if you're a member) and you'll drink for free. If you bring in 30 people they'll grill hot dogs for you in the back yard. Eat your heart out, Judge Smails.

Dive Bar Rating

NEW YORK CITY'S BEST DIVE BARS

Cherry Tavern

441 East 6th St (1st Ave and Avenue A)
Transit: F, M to 2nd Ave; L to 1st Ave   *(212) 777-1448*

I have been to dozens of East Village dive bars, and I find Cherry Tavern to be the horniest. (Doc Holliday's is a close second.) Everyone here seems to have come for the express purpose of hooking up, or finding someone to hook up with. The ceiling is covered with soundproofing foam, probably because the upstairs neighbors were complaining about the moaning. Red bulbs dangle from above, and cheesy early-'00s radio rock of the Three Doors Down, Puddle of Mud variety plays on the jukebox. (This, unfortunately, is the closest thing white folks have to baby-making R&B.) People who don't have any idea how to play pool are doing so simply for the opportunity to goose their partner when she bends over, and even the bartender seems to be making eyes.

If you're not interested in finding romance, Cherry Tavern offers cocktails like Che's Iced Tea, which is mint iced tea and bourbon, and Moscow Lemonade, which is cherry vodka and lemonade. But other than those concoctions I couldn't find any traces of a Communist influence; I mean, they also offer an Old Glory special, which is a PBR and a shot of whiskey for $4.

Other than the sex pheromones in the air, the atmosphere ain't much: Wood paneling, double-exposed photos of drunk people, a plastic orange gun hanging from the coat hook. Monday night is iPod night, says a sign: if you bring yours in, they'll play it. But folks here clearly aren't much into music appreciation. (Hence the aught rock.) They're more into the appreciation of a nice round behind, particularly one shaped by a tight pair of jeans.

Dive Bar Rating

Cordato's

94 1/2 Greenwich St (Rector Street and Carlisle St)

Transit: 1 to Rector St; R, W to Rector St; 4,5 to Broadway   *(212) 233-1573*

Formerly known for pizza, lap dances and prostitutes, Cordato's now appears to have settled into a new identity as a begrimed, low-rent watering hole. If you want to see horrendous-looking semi-naked women, go next door to the Pussycat Lounge, but if you simply want to drink at a spot where there's no chance you'll run into someone you know, Cordato's is your place.

New York Magazine called it the city's best dive bar in 2006, which is preposterous, but the people at the official-periodical-of-every-thing-that's-annoying-about-New-York were understandably proud of themselves for discovering it. Located behind a normal-looking, totally-serviceable deli, there's absolutely nothing to indicate it's lurking in the rear. Once you pass through the back door, the atmosphere completely changes, however; dirty south rap videos play on the television, the proprietor flirts/trades insults with the Puerto Rican bartender, and people stop in just long enough to order bizarre drinks. When I was there a guy asked for tequila mixed with vodka and Red Bull, which the barkeep happily whipped up for him, with ice. Later, a guy who looked like he could have been the bouncer at the Pussycat Lounge ordered three shots of Jose Cuervo, which he drank one after another, like water.

Cordato's walls are blue, the bar is plastic and the bathroom looks to have been destroyed by a category five urine hurricane. While the place was clearly originally envisioned as a swanky lounge, you can only attract so many high rollers to a tiny bar located behind a deli. For now it seems to mainly serve folks who feel most comfortable when they're slightly terrified. But then again, I was a little out of my element. For many people, the flirty Boricua imparts, it's their "secret spot." No worries—it will remain so.

Dive Bar Rating 🍾🍾🍾🍾🍾

Crehan's Pub

41-04 31st Avenue (41st Street)
Transit: R, G to Steinway St   718-728-9652

The awning that hangs over the front of Crehan's Pub features the image of a leprechaun guzzling a bottle 'o beer with both hands. The patrons inside are equally refined. A guy with no front teeth wearing a dirty Hard Rock Café sweatshirt and sweatpants asked me and my friend Matt if we wanted to play pool. We said sure. The Hard Rock guy recruited a lady friend to play with him. We shared a stick with her, and she was aggressively coached by a Vietnam vet with a handlebar mustache. "Don't chalk the cue before they use it!" Handlebar demanded. He was a middle-aged, skuzzy dude wearing gold chains and a 9-11 memorial patch on his jacket.

A younger, tree trunk of a man also looked on. Whenever anyone was about to shoot he would yell "You suck!" It was all in good fun, though, and Matt and I won the first game somehow. The trouble didn't really start until after the second game. I'm not exactly sure what happened, but Handlebar later claimed that Tree Trunk said to him, "All the niggers who died in Vietnam were cowards." This caused Handlebar to go after Tree Trunk, first with a bar stool and then with his fists.

Tree Trunk didn't really fight back at first. In fact, he apologized for his comment. But after Handlebar started taunting him—"Have you ever killed a person in your life? I have!"—Tree Trunk flew off the handle. He charged at Handlebar, only briefly deterred by another drunk from the bar who climbed onto his back to try to slow him down. Tree Trunk simply carried him along, and it took the rest of the bar intervening to stave off a beating. "Fuckin' asshole!" Tree Trunk yelled as he stormed out.

So, that's what happened at Crehan's Pub when I was there. After the confrontation, everyone talked in low voices while Handlebar got some paper towels from the bathroom and wiped off his sweaty face. "I got a get-out-of-jail-free card from the cops in the neighborhood anyway," he imparted.

Dive Bar Rating 🍾🍾🍾🍾🍾

Crocodile Lounge

325 E 14th St (1st Ave & 2nd Ave)

Transit: L to 1st Ave   *(212) 477-7747*

Free pizza with your drink? On first thought it seems too good to be true, and on second thought, you suspect the quality of the pizza. Actually, the eight-inch-wide cheese pies are completely serviceable, good in the way that all New York pizza is good, although the crust is a bit rough, and toppings are extra. Along with its sister pizza pubs on Bedford Avenue in Williamsburg (Charleston Bar & Grill), on Metropolitan Avenue in South Williamsburg (Alligator Lounge) and on Franklin Street in Greenpoint (Alligator Lounge II), the Crocodile thrives on a good gimmick and an atmosphere that's just whimsical enough to forgive the bar's status as an emerging chain.

The ceilings are low and the heat pipes shimmy along the ceiling just inches away from your head. But the Crocodile goes back forever, from the front window's nook to the sweaty pizza kitchen to the patio, accessed through an inspired game room. It features ski ball, a photo booth and driving game "Cruis'n Exotica," so named, apparently, because your travels take you to curious parts of Asia populated by bikinied chicks with sunglass-wearing parrots on their shoulders. There's also a horrible game called "Stacker," in which you attempt to line up blue cubes to win prizes ranging from High School Musical key chains to Flip video cameras.

(Why I always get to the final stage but can never win that damn camera is, well, not really beyond me, I suppose.) In any case, it's better to stay up front and save your money by eating the free pizza. I consumed mine atop a ripped pleather chair and stared at the sea-green tile on the bar, next to a girl in red fishnet stockings who was drinking well martinis. The rest of the young clientele is similarly unpretentious; rowdy, at times, and loud, perhaps excited to be getting something gratis.

Dive Bar Rating

Cubbyhole

281 W 12th St (4th St & Greenwich Ave)   *cubbyholebar.com*

Transit: A ,C,E to 14th St; L to 8th Ave; 1,2,3,F, M to 14th St   *(212) 243-9041*

A woman I talked to at the Cubbyhole didn't have much coherent to say about her own sexuality. The girl she was with was a "friend" and she herself was in the market for a hubby, so long as he was older, wealthier, well-educated and shared her political background. Oddly, she kept complaining about her lack of "gaydar." She didn't realize, for example, that the guys with the thin mustaches weren't hitting on her, they were just being friendly. And the fact that the bar was otherwise filled almost entirely with women didn't seem significant to her, either. The Cubbyhole is a "fusion" bar, she kept insisting, not like a Tex Mex sushi joint but rather a place where all sorts of people, from all sorts of orientations and neighborhoods, gather to carouse.

The bar's web site uses this "fusion" term, too, and its reviews stress that anybody is welcome. But most people would call it a Village lesbian bar. Heidi Montag's Playboy sits on a counter and the jukebox plays Lady Gaga, Madonna, Kylie Minogue, Janet Jackson and Katy Perry on repeat ("I Kissed A Girl," natch). Both the men's and women's restrooms are adorned with a frolicking, naked female goddess of some sort.

There is plenty of carousing, too, though it's hard to take yourself too seriously when you're sitting on Bugs Bunny and Daffy Duck stools and ten tons of bright plastic shit hangs from the ceiling. There's everything from leprechauns, stars and pinwheels to Chinese lanterns and a lunch box from Cape Cod. As Anna says, the spot is "dressed like a piñata." The barkeeps have been known to let favored customers (wo)man the bar while they run out for smoke breaks. All things considered, I would imagine you don't need good gaydar to have a fabulous time at the Cubbyhole.

Dive Bar Rating

WEST VILLAGE, MANHATTAN

NEW YORK CITY'S BEST DIVE BARS

Denny's Steak Pub

106 Beverley Rd

Transit: F, G to Church　　　　　　　　　　　　　　*(718) 435-2156*

KENSINGTON, BROOKLYN

Locals are afraid of Denny's Steak Pub, and proprietor Kevin Ryan knows it. Though he characterizes his establishment as a "neighborhood place," he admits he's hoping to diversify the clientele and bring in some younger, less threatening types. As it is, greasy bums smoke their cigarettes in the entryway—causing Ryan to sometimes incur fines from the city—while a trashy white guy talking with an obese lesbian does shots of Gray Goose and drops n-bombs. When his black acquaintance comes into the bar, the honky calls him a "monkey" and everybody cringes. No blows are exchanged—in fact, the pair hug a few minutes later—but it does make for some uncomfortable moments.

Ryan's now-deceased father Denny founded the establishment in Park Slope, and it moved to Kensington in 1975. The place used to sport a full menu (including steak), but nowadays they don't serve food, although Ryan brings in lesser catered entrees like pepper steak covered in black gravy and limp bell pepper slices. Not very appetizing, but you can't beat the price (free) and you can't beat the two-for-one happy hour special between five and seven, either. Ryan seems pretty desperate about getting folks in here, after all.

A couple of other bars in this diverse residential neighborhood—which features Indians, Russian Jews, Chinese, Italians and Irish—recently closed, leaving Denny's as pretty much the last of the Mohicans. I hope the place hangs on. It's got an attractive stone façade, and nice touches like brick arches along the wall, a '50s style cash register, and a winning sign: "Denny's Sports Bar, Den of Delinquents." Also, my friend Jess found Ryan—a retired firefighter in his early 50s who wears a goatee—attractive, and an 85-year-old World War II vet at the end of the bar had some funny stories to share. He said he and his buddies used to drink in Kensington until the bars closed at 4 a.m. and then drive across two rivers to Hoboken, where they'd drink until the bars closed at 6 a.m. Then they'd come back to Brooklyn, where the bars had reopened.

A pleasant, if likely apocryphal, yarn, and enough to drown out the honky complaining about bitches being nothing but hoes and tricks. Meanwhile, "Desolation Row" was playing on the jukebox. I can't make this stuff up.

Dive Bar Rating　🍾🍾🍾

NEW YORK CITY'S BEST DIVE BARS

Desmond's Tavern

433 Park Ave South (29th St & 30th St)

Transit: 6 to 28th St; R, W to 28th St (212) 684-9472

Desmond's Tavern is a wheezing, wrinkled alcoholic who no longer has the disposition to keep himself clean shaven. From the scratched faux-wood bar to the moldy air to the mildewed "Positively No Checks Cashed" sign, the place is a mess. I visited in late June, yet crusty Cinco de Mayo leis still hung behind the bar. The back room was done up in St. Patrick's Day decorations. St. Patrick's Day 1998, I'm guessing.

Located on an oddly-slummy stretch of Park Avenue South near a Subway sandwich shop, Desmond's is ostensibly an Irish Pub. The aging bartender, after all, speaks with a thick Irish accent and spills his pint while talking. He's a thrill to look at, in any case—full comb over, double chin, giant bushy eyebrows, missing teeth, the whole works. He hums along to "Janie's Got A Gun" while setting the cash box on the bar and adding money from the register. (I hope he's got his own gun.)

Desmond's boasts an international flavor, sort of. Its four or five televisions all featured different sports, from the Mets game to a rugby match to an Argentinean soccer game, which was being played in the sand. (No, I don't know why it was being played in the sand.) Apparently Desmond's draws a decent lunch crowd, but don't go there for dinner. They stop serving a full menu at six, although you can still get fish and chips and the like on some nights. There's live music on weekends occasionally, but during the weeknights it's pretty bleak. When I was there the clientele consisted of an old man in a toupee and sunglasses, a couple of young professional guys who kept threatening to start a drinking contest, and a chubby guy playing Golden Tee. I left feeling pretty good about myself.

Dive Bar Rating 🍾🍾🍾🍾🍾

The Distinguished Wakamba Cocktail Lounge

543 8th Avenue (37th St & 38th St)

Transit: A,C,E to 34th St; A,C,E, 1,2,3,Q,N,R, S, 7 to 42nd   *(212) 244-9045*

Located on the outskirts of Times Square, The Distinguished Wakamba Cocktail Lounge recalls New York the way it was before Bloomberg and Giuliani scrubbed it clean. An undercover cop killed an unarmed guy in front of the place a while back, and it's surrounded by a White Castle, a Papaya Dog, a Dunkin Donuts, a porn store and another porn store. Both of the latter establishments had ads for *Pirates: Stagnetti's Revenge*, starring Jesse Jane. With a budget of $8 million, it's the most expensive adult film of all time.

Who pays fifty bucks to own a movie like that? Probably the same type of person who knowingly orders a cocktail at The Distinguished Wakamba Cocktail Lounge. I won't say how expensive they are—just don't do it. Beers are five dollars, four at happy hour, so just drink beer.

Despite the fake palm trees and the net on the ceiling harboring plastic fish, the Wakamba is not a tiki bar. "Is this a tiki bar?" I asked the bartender, a blonde of Eastern European birth, who was wearing more clothes than Wakamba beermaids usually do. "No, it's a Spanish bar," she said. I found that hard to believe—did I mention the place has tiki torches?—but the fact that they don't make tiki drinks confirmed her claim.

Still, there weren't any Latin people when my wife Anna and I were there, just blacks and whites who had picked through the jukebox's Shakira and Alejandro Sanz to find the Guns N' Roses. Thankfully it was *Use Your Illusion* GN'R, which, for my money beats the beejesus out of *Appetite for Destruction*. For starters, there's simply twice as much music. And that trilogy of power ballads…Muaw!

After we left, I had to run back in because I'd forgotten my bag, briefly stranding Anna on the corner. In my absence, a local hornball walked by and sized her up. "Nice," he said.

Dive Bar Rating

Doc Holliday's

141 Avenue A (9th St & St Marks Place)

(212) 979-0312   *Transit: L to 1st Ave*

Doc Holliday's is rockabilly from head to toe, I think. Cheeky and flirty, it's got cowboy boots dangling upside down from the ceiling, Chuck Berry's "Reelin' and Rockin'" on the juke and girls in bangs and dresses dancing next to the pool table. The hand-written, scotch-taped sign on the men's room door indicates that the facilities belong to "Elvis," and an arrow pointing to the door handle notes that it is "Elvis' Knob." There are steer horns and a mounted buck's head on the wall draped with Mardi Gras beads. Are Mardi Gras beads rockabilly? In circumstances like these, perhaps.

Our bartendress had pale skin, dark hair pulled back and a form-fitting, strapless dress in the pin-up girl style. She reeled off about a dozen drink specials when we saddled up. Maud, Jeff and I settled on miniscule gin and tonics for three bucks, and combos of Genesee Cream Ale cans and shots of well whisky for five. We then proceeded to get knocked backwards by the cheap booze; despite claiming the "Flavor of a fine ale and the smoothness of a premium lager," Genesee's most notable quality is that it tastes warm and flat even after lengthy periods of refrigeration.

Owing to the utilitarian brands of liquors Doc Holliday's specializes in—a neon sign behind the bar advertises Pucker—it's not surprising that the place is a bit banged up. The floors are sloped, and a piece of particle board looks like it harbored a dart board until someone bashed it in with a baseball bat. Next to that is a box containing dozens and dozens of red pool chalk blocks. Again, I'm not exactly sure if that's rockabilly, but I'm willing to bet that it is.

Dive Bar Rating

Don Pedro's

90 Manhattan Ave (Boerum St and Mckibbin St)

Transit:J,M to Lorimer St; L to Montrose Ave; G to Broadway   *(718) 218-6914*

For an unkempt East Williamsburg hole in the wall near the Bushwick border, Don Pedro's wears a lot of hats. By night, it's a small-but-beloved concert venue, one that features everything from punk and indie acts to Raya Brass Band, an "NYC Balkan/Eastern European Wedding and Party Band." By day, it's a first-rate Ecuadorian restaurant, known for plantains, goat meat stew and cow feet soup. (Note that the eatery is only open from 11 a.m. to 6 p.m.)

At all times, however, it's a charming dive bar, well-worth visiting even if you're not hungry or going to see a show. For starters, they're practically giving away cans of Rolling Rock—$2 before ten, and 2 for $5 the rest of the time—and they've also got a "Rot Gut" special (PBR and a shot for $6) and nips of Colt 45. The front awning, tables, and dilapidated booths are a hallucination of primary hues, and the color frenzy continues in the back hall, which features terrifying abstract paintings of African dictators like Mugabe. Barfly entertainment includes old-time cinema on a small, pull-down screen, classics like *Attack Of the Giant Leeches*.

Sadly, times are tough at Don Pedro's; they're reportedly cutting employee hours. When I was there, a twenty-something girl in brown boots burst into the joint, apologizing to the owner for being late. (Apparently, black car drivers don't know how to find the place.) She then began setting up for her bar shift, only to have to abandon her post when the evening's music group showed up. It seems that employees are responsible both for pouring drinks and running the sound, and in fact can only procure shifts when they've booked a band.

One hopes the spot isn't a victim of the recession. Its DIY spirit, flamboyant appearance and affordable elixirs represent much of what makes NYC great.

Dive Bar Rating

Dublin House

225 West 79th St (Amsterdam Ave & Broadway)

Transit: 1 to 79th St

(212) 874-9528

The clientele at Dublin House says a lot of dumb things. For example: "I don't know if you know this about your dear best friend," an overweight brunette sitting near me said to a guy who may have been her boyfriend, "but he makes the best Irish car bombs I've ever had in my life." Even I said something stupid (imagine that), at least in the mind of the silver-haired bartender, who had a thick Irish accent. "Got any cheap beer?" I asked. "It's all cheap!" he said, throwing a coaster in front of me. "Six dollars for a pint of Guinness. Best price in Manhattan. Where you from, Kansas City?" He poured my beer, set it down with a slam, and then walked to the other end of the bar.

His saltiness—or gusto, if you prefer—was probably a bit over the top, but I have to admit he runs a tight ship. Dublin House is immaculately clean and impeccably kept, from the long, glistening bar to the wood-paneled walls to the bathroom, which is less than half the size of the towering red and green neon harp sign that sits out front, flashing.

The bar's most charming trait is its intimacy. The ceilings are low and the booths are tiny, just large enough to squeeze one person on either side of a table. You may not even realize at first that there's a back room, absolutely crammed with furniture, which the regulars have to themselves.

Eventually, the bartender came back over to my end of the bar, saw I wasn't done with my drink yet, scowled, and moved on to the hefty brunette and her maybe boyfriend. He served their drinks, and then took some bills from the pile they had sitting on the bar. Efficient, clean, and cozy, that's Dublin House. Just try not to say anything stupid.

Dive Bar Rating

Duff's Brooklyn

168 Marcy Ave (South 5th St & Broadway)   *duffsbrooklyn.com*

Transit: J,M,Z to Marcy Ave   *(718) 599-2092*

When I heard Duff's Brooklyn was a heavy metal bar I wasn't enthused, as I've never been into Slayer, Metallica and the like. But when I arrived and quickly realized it was actually a cock rock bar, I smiled. Whitesnake's "Slide It In" was playing on the sound system, and the succession of acts that followed (Lita Ford, Kix, etc.) convinced me that Duff's was the domain of hair metal fans, of which I am proudly one. Sure, the genre that dominated air waves during my late '80s and early '90s pre-adolescence doesn't get a lot of respect, but I will put the production on those White Lion, Europe and Cinderella albums up against anything.

Duff's original incarnation was as the Bellevue Bar in Hell's Kitchen, and it moved to this spot by the JMZ Marcy stop a few years back. A red neon sign in the window promises "Thrills!" and the interior boasts a carnival atmosphere, complete with chili pepper lights and a cage in the back room harboring a straight-jacket clad mannequin. The bathroom doors say "Bastids" and "Bitches" and horror movie posters line the walls next to lacquered cue cards from a short-lived MTV program. "Welcome to Extreme Rock, a brand new show where I'll get to show you some of the hardest rock videos on MTV," the cards say. "I'm Rob Zombie and for the next hour I'll be hanging out at the extreme rock hangout Bellevue Bar in NYC."

Duff's has at least a couple of mascots, including Lemmy Kilmister Duff, a black and white cat who sits calmly on a bar stool. Then there's Dancin' Dominick, a retired postal worker and former employee, whom Duff's owner discovered while Dominick was dancing alone in the Virgin Records at Times Square. Known for his kung-fu chop moves and suits with a flower in the lapel, he died in 2002 but lives on through stickers of his face that are plastered in every corner of the bar.

Dive Bar Rating

PACMAN/GALAGA

Welcome to the Johnson's

Parkside Lounge

Hank's Saloon

Raccoon Lodge

Red Hook Bait & Tackle

Stacks Tavern

Ear Inn

326 Spring St (Greenwich St and Washington St)
Transit: C,E to Spring St; 1 to Houston

(212) 226-9060

The Ear Inn is one of the oldest drinkeries in town. Of that we can be fairly certain, but the rest of its history is a bit unclear. According to its own, surely-not-entirely-accurate accounting of its past, the place was built inside the townhouse of an African-American aide to George Washington named James Brown, someone who is "perhaps pictured" in the famous painting of Washington crossing the Delaware. Brown later found success in New York's tobacco trade and moved here to the "suburbs," i.e. modern day SoHo. His house, with its largely-unchanged wooden frame and brick façade, is on the National Register of Historic Buildings.

The house eventually became a bar, the backyard was turned into a dining room and the joint functioned as a speakeasy during prohibition. The apartment upstairs, meanwhile, was variously used as a brothel, boarding house and smuggler's den. Ghosts apparently still haunt the place, which was never given a proper name. In 1977, the spot's new owners sought to avoid the lengthy process of review the Landmark Commission imposed on new signs, and so they simply painted over their existing neon "BAR" sign to read "EAR," in honor of an eponymous magazine next door.

Who knows what's true and what's not, but to be sure Ear Inn is a great spot with a great sign. It's got excellent food, including burger and salmon plates for under $11, and steak with mashed potatoes and salad for $13. But it also possesses the soul of a dive, what with the cluttered bar hogging most of the space in the front room—there is barely space for the two small televisions amidst the clutter and bric-a-brack. Beer coasters have been proudly taped up like Boy Scout merit badges, and above the bar is a veritable alchemists' set of dusty jugs, bottles and other assorted glassware, all reportedly dug up from the backyard-cum-dining room. Like a trip to Boston or Philadelphia, having a beer here feels like witnessing American history, even if the details of said history aren't exactly clear.

Dive Bar Rating

NEW YORK CITY'S BEST DIVE BARS

Farrell's

215 Prospect Park West (16th Street)
Transit: F to 15th St (718) 788-8779

I had a hard time getting a drink at Farrell's, what with the moat of beer in the front room. After tiptoeing to the side of the bar and ordering, I asked the barkeep if there had been an accident. "Yeah, drunken firemen," he said, by way of explanation. Like almost everyone else here he was goateed and pudgy, and looked like he could have been a fireman himself. He grabbed a bunch of newspapers and pushed them around on the floor with his shoe. This had the effect of improving the situation… not at all. He eventually gave up, threw the wet papers in the garbage and went back behind the bar, resuming his chat with a couple of dudes who must have been cops, because they were complaining about having to appear in court.

"I got grand jury tomorrow," said one.

"That sucks balls!" said the other.

I waded into the back room. The atmosphere was similar to what I'd imagine an Elks Lodge's would be: stately, with a deco-style tin ceiling and sturdy slabs of heavily-lacquered wood harboring mirrors. The drinking customs also seemed Elks-like, except instead of chugging ale from glass steins, Farrell's customers use Styrofoam cups, dozens of which are stacked behind the bar. These quart servings of lager are called "Farrellizers." Are they tastier than your average glass of beer in a Styrofoam cup? Could be. A message board commentator posits that Farrell's brass taps are especially cold, leading to an improved quality in the suds they dispense.

It's said that the recently-arrived, moneyed Windsor Terrace transplants hate Farrell's, perhaps because its patrons tend to deposit their non-biodegradable drinking containers on the sidewalk when they leave. But there's no reason the pub's patrons have to butt heads with the new guard, who are, after all, supposed to be famous for their tolerance. The newbies would be wise to find out what getting Farrellized is all about.

Dive Bar Rating

Fish Bar

237 East 5th Street (2nd Ave and Cooper Square)
Transit: 6 to Astor Place;R to 8th St;F to 2nd Ave　　　*(212) 475-4949*

During your first drink, a glass of red wine, perhaps, Fish Bar has a beatnik vibe. The bartender wears a fedora and a goatee, Japanese lanterns hang from the ceiling and some of the tables double as backgammon and chess boards. You half expect someone to pull an upright bass out of their knapsack and start complaining that the best minds of their generation were hallucinating Arkansas and Blake-like tragedy among the scholars of war.

During your second drink, probably a pale lager, you begin to feel like you're on a forgotten seaside strip next to the Gulf of Mexico. The walls are splashed with bright blue paint, and airbrushed coral and sharks loom to your left and right. Soft soul music plays overhead, and it's not hard to imagine yourself killing time in a dingy Key West tavern waiting on a source who's going to spill the beans about a massive narcotics trafficking ring that Jeb Bush is somehow caught up in.

By your third and fourth drinks, probably a PBR and shot of well-bourbon combo that, at seven bucks, costs two dollars more than in most East Village dive bars but forget that for a minute, you've lost your buzz because a large group of international students have come in. The room is small and square and the walls are made of concrete, so you're subjected to every word these morons have to say about politics and climate change.

You find the bathroom, which has a picture of an old, horny, Zeus-like Merman on the door, and duck inside. As you stare into the mirror you find yourself somehow burning for the ancient heavenly connection to the starry dynamo in the machinery of night. Or whatever.

Dive Bar Rating 🍾🍾

Frank's Cocktail Lounge

660 Fulton St (Ashland Place & Fort Greene Place)

Transit 2, 3, 4, 5, M, N, Q, W, R, B, D to Atlantic Ave-Pacific St   *(718) 625-9339*

I got to Frank's before the after-work rush and asked the suave, older bartender if she had any happy hour specials. After a long pause she turned her head away from *Notorious*, the Biggie Smalls biopic that was playing on the big screen in the back, its sound competing with TV news broadcasts on either side of the bar.

"Tell me what you want," she said. "I'll set you up."

"What do you make that's good?"

"Everything I make is good!" Irritated, she gestured behind her at the Christmas-light ringed, mirror-backed bar. "We've got all sorts of liquor."

"Make me something sweet," I said, before glancing at the glowing bottles of Hypnotiq and blue, mango and red colored Alize occupying prime real estate. "But not too sweet."

She made me a cranberry and gin, then turned back to *Notorious*, to an explicit sex scene where Biggie fucks a girl he just picked up off the street.

My friend Steve arrived and ordered a Manhattan. "Can you hold a Manhattan?" the bartender asked, tilting her head. This may have been a comment on his skinny frame, who knows. It was kind of bitchy, but she pulled it off. Her eye shadow and form-fitting top were the same color as the Hypnotiq.

Steve nodded, looked at me curiously, and put some R. Kelly on the jukebox. A wise move, even though it was now competing with *Notorious* and the TV news. That's how one creates a mood at Frank's, after all. It's not a traditional dive bar; it isn't gross and the drinks aren't cheap. But the stucco ceiling, fans lit by festive red and yellow colored lights and occasional live jazz create some serious atmosphere. It's a comfortable place for old black folks in a neighborhood increasingly filled with young, white ones. The latter should be ready for a little abuse.

Dive Bar Rating

Freddy's Bar & Backroom

485 Dean Street (6th Avenue and Flatbush Ave)
Transit 2, 3, 4, 5, M, N, Q, W, R, B, D to Atlantic Ave-Pacific St   (718) 622-7035

Author's note: On May 1, 2010, Freddy's hosted its own farewell party. The state used eminent domain to evict the bar, in favor of the new Nets stadium. "Fuck you, Jay-Z, " said everybody. Freddy's has now moved to a new location, but I decided to memorialize the original spot by leaving in this entry.

Everyone who's been to Freddy's recommends it. One girl told me she worried about becoming a "Fred-hag" because she spent so much time there. The spiritual home of the Atlantic Yards/Nets stadium opposition is stuffed with young, sociable folks, especially on the weekends.

Why does everybody like it so much? Perhaps for the mounted jack-rabbit's head, or the illuminated red sign in front of the men's room showing a guy peeing on the floor. Maybe they dig the video art montages, which show mashed-up kung-fu movies, porn and vintage commercials. Perhaps attendees enjoy the live music performed in the raucous-yet-intimate backroom, or else they just want to puff, as around 2 am, the place regularly turns into a smoking bar.

I personally like it for the creepy aquarium. My friend Tal said I should check it out because, despite having coral, fake botanicals, an oxygenator and rocks, it was devoid of living creatures. That wasn't true, I saw upon closer inspection. On the left side of the tank were a couple of white bottomfeeder fish and a giant, nearly translucent one. At the tank's bottom right side sat a large, white albino frog, eyes popped open and motionless. I nearly shrieked.

I asked a passerby if it was real.

"Yes," he said. "And it's dead."

The female bartender, wearing an asymmetrical, one-strapped halter top, denied both that the animal was an albino frog, and that it was dead. "It's a…something," she said, a bit confused.

Another bartender countered that our little friend was indeed an albino frog, and that he was very much alive. "They just sit there like that," he said. "For hours."

Dive Bar Rating 🍾🍾🍾

Grassroots Tavern

20 St. Marks Place (2nd and 3rd Avenue)

Transit: 6 to Astor Place; R to 8th St; L to 3rd Ave   *(212) 475-9443*

If you took the Grassroots Tavern, put it on a flatbed truck and deposited it in a small Nebraska or Wyoming town, it would probably serve aspiring cowboys who were late on their child support. But seeing that it's in the heart of downtown's collegiate vortex, it's almost exclusively the domain of binge-drinking co-eds, recent graduates slumming and a few middle-aged bohemian lowlifes.

Proudly ratty, this thirty-five-year-old St. Marks Place institution has a low tin ceiling, and anyone taller than six feet should worry about bumping his or her head. In many places, the ceiling sags, as if the upstairs could come crashing in at any moment. (A few rickety wooden columns don't seem to offer much support.) Only a sadist would fire up the juke box here, as the noise is deafening whenever the place is crowded, which is always. Folks are drawn by the dinge and the drink prices; many pints are just three or four bucks, with a dollar knocked off during happy hour. The elegant, slightly-aloof barkeep mainly dispenses plastic pitchers, however, which are proudly hung behind the bar when not in use, a good indication of the joint's décor style. There's also a wooden phone booth, a trio of dartboards in the back, and a popcorn machine that may have been last washed during the Carter administration. The lighting is low, the tables are deeply-etched with graffiti, and seemingly-alive dust clumps sit atop the air conditioning vents.

The truth is, if you're over thirty you might want to skip the Grassroots Tavern and head east to Holiday Cocktail Lounge, where you're more likely to leave with your hearing intact. But if you happen to be young, dumb and full of cum, I can't think of a better place for ya.

Dive Bar Rating

Greenpoint Tavern

188 Bedford Ave (6th Street & 7th Street)

Transit: L to Bedford Ave   *(718) 384-9539*

Not long ago, someone was assaulting drunk hipsters roaming the streets of Williamsburg late at night and stealing their money. Though surely traumatizing for those involved, the story was satisfying to many. When it comes to the trendy and privileged, after all, people tend to double up on the schadenfreude. Those who bemoan the gentrification of the neighborhood might even imagine the assailant a ghost from Williamsburg's past, seeking vigilante justice.

One suspects the mugger would avoid denizens of the Greenpoint Tavern, however. Sure, it's located in the heart of the Bedford Avenue beast, across the street from the L stop and sharing a strip with countless cool kid bars. And, yeah, it's got something of an ironic feel, what with its plethora of "Gone For A Smoke" cardboard coasters and ageless owners Rosemary and Bill camped out at the end of the bar. She sips beer from a brandy glass, he nods like a maniac, and Teddy the burly bartender decorates the place obscenely every holiday. When I was there with my friend Lavinia, giant paper mache eggs hung from the ceiling, the walls were lined with pastel bunnies and the bar was draped in Easter-themed Christmas lights.

But the clientele is mostly unironic, whether it's the working stiffs paying close attention to *Wheel of Fortune* or townies like the guy I sat next to. He wore an unfashionable goatee and a face of smoker's wrinkles, and his teeth looked to be the kind you pop out. There were only five of them on the top row, you see, and they were clustered at the front. Drinking quickly from $3.50 Styrofoam quarts of Bud Light, he told me his entire professional life story, from the time federal marshals raided his pirate New Kids On The Block t-shirt silk screening operation, to his work as an electrical contractor, to his plans to enroll in a Gotham Writing class to become a writer. It bored the shit out of me, but he listened to my story too, and when we were done he congratulated me by name and promised to buy this book when it came out. So thank you, townie guy, for your support. And I'm sorry I was too much of a carpetbagging hipster to catch your name.

Dive Bar Rating ▮ ▮ ▮

Hank's Saloon

46 3rd Ave (Atlantic Ave & Pacific St)　　　*www.exitfive.com/hankssaloon*

Transit: 2, 3, 4, 5, M, N, Q, W, R, B, D to Atlantic Ave-Pacific St　　*(718) 625-8003*

You'll know Hank's Saloon by the flames painted on the side of the building and the doorway, which doubles as a portal transporting you back in time to a Lubbock, Texas road house, circa 1965. The musicians on-stage are ladies in paisley dresses playing archtop guitars and banjos, and guys in shades and boots playing drums and upright bass. Hank's Cheap Beer is on tap, Red Hook Beef Jerky is for sale and a giant American flag is draped behind the bar.

Between sets "Gin and Juice" comes on the overhead speakers— The Gourds version, of course. Anyone trying to get to the bar will need to doggy paddle their way through a sea of Pabst-clasping young co-eds, flirting brunettes and blondes with giant hair getting up off of their boyfriend's (or whoever's) laps to stretch their legs. Those who are single will be in their element, and those who aren't had better keep tabs on their significant others. If you go to use the men's room be careful because the door doesn't close very quickly. This means that if you're standing at the urinal, the ladies outside have a good solid twenty seconds or more to witness you doing your thing. Is this a big problem? No, because, as that great country-western purveyor of Texan wisdom once said, "There will never be another tonight." Okay, so maybe that was Bryan Adams. Who cares? After a night of stomping honky tonk and a few Hank's Cheap, you're not going to know your ass from your armpit anyway.

Dive Bar Rating　

NEW YORK CITY'S BEST DIVE BARS

Holiday Cocktail Lounge

75 St. Marks Pl (1st Ave & 2nd Ave)

Transit: 6 to Astor; L to 1st Ave; R to 8th St   *(212) 777-9637*

For the most part, St. Marks Place should be avoided. While there are some good restaurants there, they're usually packed, and the street often feels like a hippie version of Times Square. The only difference is that instead of being overrun by Argentines trying to find the Empire State Building, it's full of pierced teenage runaways trying to find dope. The sidewalks are often so crowded you can't walk in a straight line, and the Henna salespeople, Gyro stands and glass pipe artisans cater almost exclusively to the stoned.

But though Holiday Cocktail Lounge is on St. Marks Place, it's not of St. Marks Place. Slightly subterranean, it never seems to be full, even on Saturday nights, when Kris Kristofferson sings "Me and Bobby McGee" on the jukebox and a small blonde woman with a squeaky voice takes your orders. Cocktails are $4, which is the correct price, and they are served in four-inch tall, cylindrical glasses, which are the correct glasses to serve cocktails in.

An inviting horseshoe bar draped in kitschy knick knacks wraps the joint's front room, and the walls are covered with decaying and ironic signs and advertisements, like the one from Brut deodorant that reads: "Makes armpit farts smell great." Since the old Ukrainian owner Steven Lutak died, the place has added a couple of flat screen televisions, but it has retained the wood-paneled walls, pleather booths and linoleum floor. It remains a haven for New Yorkers who happen to find themselves stuck on St. Marks Place.

Dive Bar Rating

Holland Bar

532 9th Ave (9th St and 40th St)

Transit: A,C,E to 42ndSt/Port Authority   *(212) 502-4609*

Some people complain that Manhattan has been turned into Disneyland, but there are pockets of Hell's Kitchen that feel, appropriately, more like Hades.

On a steamy May night at the Holland Bar, a general contractor named Albert was telling Anna and me about how he'd gone through a lot of shit in his life. Much of it owed to that fact that he grew up in bad Brooklyn neighborhoods and took pride in his race. He wore a baseball cap with glittering dollar signs on it, backwards sunglasses and Timberlands. A "wigger," you might have called him, but he said he liked not just hip hop, but also Led Zeppelin, Ozzy Osbourne and "freestyle," a type of electronic music popular in the '80s. His tattoos included a pair of tear drops near his left eye, a spider web over his elbow and other Aryan-themed ink beneath his clothes. He nonetheless got along swimmingly with Jeff, the black bartender, who didn't remove him even after he knocked over somebody's beer with an unsteady paw. This was only his fourth drink, Albert pleaded. Here, that is. Truth be told, he'd been drinking since noon, twelve solid hours. It would have been longer, but at 10 am, a deli employee informed him he couldn't buy booze yet because it was Sunday. "I'll die if I have to wait until then," he joked (but not really). Fortunately he now had a bottle stashed in his bag to help him wind down later.

The recently-reopened Holland Bar features one wall of exposed brick and another wall of half wainscoting, half bare dry wall. It's the kind of place that looks like it's held together with duct tape, and the bathroom door literally is. Besides a table up front the bar is the only place to sit down, and when people dance in the aisles, trying to get past them is the equivalent of cutting in. The giant, magnificently-scripted "Holland" sign behind the bar dates from the 1930s, a holdover from the joint's former incarnation as the saloon at the Holland Welfare Hotel, over on 42nd Street. The Hotel didn't survive, but the dive and the sign were transplanted here.

Before long another regular came in, a guy with the right side of his face bubbled up and nearly melted off. Despite being hard to look at, he was greeted warmly by all. Holland Bar is rough, but it's not so bad. The air circulation is decent, the people—if harboring unfortunate ideas about race—are friendly. And the help is non-judgmental.

Dive Bar Rating

Homestretch Pub

214 Kings Highway

Transit: Kings Highway (N)   *(718) 372-9719*

At the Homestretch Pub, the men are men and the women are... not in attendance. When I was there, it was strictly a sausage party, an Italian sausage party, that is, full of olive-skinned dudes in close-cropped hair wearing white sneakers and dark blue Yankees t-shirts. I went there with Dive Bar Ben, a plump, ruddy-faced scholar who lives in the neighborhood with his 82-year-old dad. Within moments of our arrival, Ben announced that I was writing a book on dive bars. One of the white sneaker guys turned around, crinkled his forehead and began rubbing his chin with two fingers. "What are you saying? You'd better give it a good write-up!" I stammered something about "best local bars," and then nearly choked on my drink when Ben added that he and I had met in a watering hole near Port Authority.

Before anyone could say anything else, Ben began chatting loudly about his ex-girlfriend, who was pregnant with their child but attempting to prohibit him from seeing the baby. They had a family court date scheduled, but his court-appointed lawyer was a dud. Whether any of this had to do with the giant bump on Ben's forehead or the red welts on his hand I wasn't sure, but he quickly squeezed down three surprisingly cheap Sapphire and tonics. Imparting that in recent weeks he'd had appointments with doctors, shrinks and a psychic—and had attended an AA class—he proceeded to pull out a bottle of anti-depressants and wash a pill down with his drink.

Dive Bar Ben may be a mess, but he sure can pick a dive bar. Homestretch Pub is a classy and clean, idiosyncratic little watering hole. A collection of hard hats hangs behind the bar, an Animal doll (from *The Muppet Show*) is handcuffed to the coat rack and the backyard patio is corralled by a chain link fence and filled with lawn furniture. In the main room, a mural running almost the length of the place is protected by a mini wrought-iron fence. Reportedly dating back forty-five years, the mural features thoroughbreds racing, and the horse theme is repeated throughout the bar, per its name.

Bensonhurst is an extremely conservative part of Brooklyn, and walking from the Kings Highway N stop I was surprised to see American flags planted in front of nearly every house on West 8th Street. There's a rolled-up flag sitting in the corner at the Homestretch, too, and a guy at the bar told us that he's not going to see the new *The Three Stooges* movie. Why? Because Sean Penn is a Communist.

Dive Bar Rating

GREAT HAPPY HOURS

Manitoba's

Grassroots Tavern

Alibi

Welcome to the Johnson's

International Bar

120 1/2 First Ave (East 7th Street and St. Marks Place)

Transit: L to 1st Ave; 6 to Astor Place; F,M to 2nd Ave (212) 777-1643

The International Bar isn't as divey as it once was, but it still gets points for surreality. When I was there a pair of ditzes in orange tube tops were pushing Jägermeister swag, to the bemusement of the older (but still randy) crowd. I wasn't interested in having a green and black lanyard draped over my neck, thanks, but plenty of other dudes were, and the free Jäger shots were a hit as well.

To go with the caramel digestif, the tall female bartender with severe bangs suggested a two dollar can of Genesee. "The cream ale?" I asked dubiously, recalling the flat swill I'd tried at Doc Holliday's. "No, not the cream ale," she curtly responded. "The cream ale tastes like shit." Indeed, the standard brew was much more satisfying, and helped me appreciate the madcap surroundings of the narrow room, which has esoteric and anime-style erotica art on the walls and an ivy-ringed patio full of chainsmokers in the back. (It doubles as a storage area for trash and various shop items.)

The other barkeep wore a sailor cap and jean skirt with a studded belt. Before leaving she kissed the cheeks of seemingly half the patrons. Next I turned my attention to a shaggy Velvet Underground reject, who began violently attempting to force his way into one of the bathrooms, having jumped a line of annoyed folks to do so. "My ex-girlfriend's in there!" he explained. When she finally emerged, he castigated her. "You fucking idiot! I was getting you a beer!" So, yes, the spot feels downright Dali-an. As I was leaving, I was handed a coupon for "Free Jäger Music," which made me wonder if the Genesee had gone to my head.

Dive Bar Rating

Irene's Pub

Intersection of Nassau and Manhattan Avenues

Transit: G to Nassau Avenue   *No phone*

You know you're out of your element when you walk into a bar and people first stare, then rearrange themselves to make room for you to sit down. It sets the tone for the evening. *You're the show.* So it went at Irene's Pub, where my wife Anna, my friend Dillon and I were told beforehand there would be old Polish men passed out on the bar. There were, as well as a Spuds Mackenzie doll, a picture of Pope John Paul II and plenty of Christmas lights. Though a sign read, "No smoking permitted in the bar"…there was, in fact, smoking in the bar.

"Mike," said the guy in the camo pants, introducing himself to us and gesticulating in a way that indicated we would be fine if we stayed with him. In his garbled English, he added that he was Slovakian—not Polish like most everyone else here—and went on to tell us about a life-changing AC/DC concert at Madison Square Garden and how the only true Americans were the Indians. He then went on a monologue intended to demonstrate the weakness of our economy. His cousin had left Slovakia sometime after the fall of the Berlin Wall and moved to Italy, you see, where he was now an ambassador. Mike, meanwhile, departed the country of his birth around the same time, but hadn't fared as well. "I…carpenter!" he cried.

He then began buying us shots of Bison Grass vodka—called ubrówka in Polish. It's sweet and minty, and the bottle has a long piece of grass in it. As soon as our glasses hit the bar he ordered another round, which I paid for. While I was in the bathroom he grabbed Anna and began dancing with her to the Europop playing on the jukebox. I came back to him spinning and dipping her. They returned to the bar and he apologized. "She, yours? So sorry. I'm idiot." Before we left he complimented her curls, "The *best*," and bought us another round of Bison Grass vodka.

I haven't been able to discern this place's exact address, and there seems to be absolutely no trace of it on the internet. Someone told us it was called "Walker's," but the bartender insisted it's called "Irena." A neon Budweiser sign on the premises, however, calls it "Irene's Pub," so let's go with that.

Dive Bar Rating 🍾🍾🍾🍾🍾

Irish Eyes

5008 Broadway (212th Street and 213th Street)

Transit: 1 to 215th St; A to 207th St   *(212) 567-9072*

You know you're in a great dive when you and your friend order two beers, and the bartender asks for four dollars. Total.

Of course, the selection at Irish Eyes could be better. They appear to have two beers on draft, but that's not actually the case. Though one of the tap's handles is red and in the shape of a pine tree, leading one to belief it dispenses Red Hook…it doesn't. "We got Bud," said Bernie the bartender, a magnificent woman from the Bronx with crimped blonde hair and bangs. "That's it."

Outside there's wood paneling. The razzle-dazzle interior, meanwhile, says "big ambition, low budget," with its ski-chalet architecture, wood grain linoleum bar, stucco ceiling, and top shelves lined with brandies and schnapps that you've never heard of. Irish Mist, anyone? Black Haus?

The place has many quirks—like the non-flushing urinals in the men's room—and is crowded with old, coughing, witty white folks, from the guy claiming that his deodorant just expired to the gravel-voiced, ponytailed old timer flirting with the ladies smoking in the doorway. Sample exchange: "Don't go home with any strange men." "They couldn't handle me!" If you hang around long enough something like the following will probably go down: The Irish music will be interrupted by Shania Twain's "Up," and everyone will sing along. A girl will come in off the street to use the pay phone, but will end up convincing Bernie to let her charge her cell behind the bar instead. While this is happening the pair will talk baseball, with Bernie explaining that her entire family is, inexplicably, Mets fans. That is, except for her, which is obvious since she's got a Yankees t-shirt tucked into her blue jeans. Still, when Daniel Murphy cranks a solo shot on the TV she won't be able to help getting caught up in the moment. "I can't believe I'm rooting for the Mets!" she'll exclaim, before refilling your beer without asking. Before the guy with the expired deodorant leaves he will tip her a few bucks, which means she can now take a cab back to the Bronx when her shift is over, instead of the bus.

Dive Bar Rating

J Mac's Lounge

600 West 57th St (ar 11th Avenue)

Transit: 1,A,B,C,D to 59th St/Columbus Circle   *No phone*

When he wasn't stepping outside to smoke menthols, the guy in the Yankees' bandana at J Mac's Lounge's bar spent most of his time chewing beef jerky. That, and enduring the nonstop chatter from the barkeep, a dark-haired lady named Jesse with a tremendously large rear end. She was great about the buybacks, for sure, but man did she talk a lot, about her family and how she had recently treated her son to a "ghetto day at the movies," paying for *Where The Wild Things Are* but then staying for a gratis twofer by ducking into *Paranormal Activities*.

The whole time she was chatting away, she was also putting on her face in the bar's mirror. This took the better part of half an hour, what with the eye shadow and the blush and the concealer. When she was done, she poured herself a Jager bomb and went outside to smoke. Suddenly the place was dead silent. It was a Monday night, and the only other people here were a young serviceman wearing big glasses and a guy in a trench coat who elected to remain standing.

J Mac's hasn't seen a dusting or a sweeping in many years. It's not really scary, just sort of dumpy. There are nice touches, though, like the antique-yet-functioning cigarette machine and the hand-drawn cartoon near the bathrooms, in which a mouse announces that he's come up with a great ad for the bar: "Come to J Mac's or we'll break your %^&@# knees!" By the end of the night I'd even come around to Jesse, who makes it a habit to hug her customers and to take personal phone calls on the job. One was from her son's teacher, and as Jesse went outside to conference she offered an apology: "I'm an active parent, see."

Dive Bar Rating

Jackie's 5th Amendment

404 5th Avenue (7th Street)
Transit:F, D,G,N,R to 4th Ave   *(718) 788-9123*

"Hi Carol, how are you?" asks the snaggle-toothed bartender of the squat Latin lady with heavily-painted eyebrows ambling through the door. Carol holds out one hand horizontally and rocks it back and forth, like a seesaw. "I don't know," she says, which is probably the most honest answer to that question. "My wife has been drinking again lately," puts in an old guy sitting at the other end of the bar. "But that's just because the doctor told her she was anemic."

Jackie's 5th Amendment is the kind of place that has one of those "Hiding From Wife" charts, detailing the costs for the bartender to cover your ass when your spouse calls in. ("$2.00 Just Missed Him," etc.) Except, at Jackie's, the chart is not really a joke. As a muscled guy in a tank top rolls out, for example, he notices that it's already an hour after he told his old lady he'd be home. "I'll just tell her the train got a flat tire," he concludes. The ceiling is stucco, and there are red mood lights above the bar. A bucket of seven ounce beers is nine bucks. There's an eight-track player behind the counter and, in the back, next to the dining area that doesn't appear to have been used in decades, an old-time Anheuser-Busch globe hangs from the ceiling. At the center of the globe is a lit-up bottle of Bud, with Clydesdales prancing around it. Near the front door there's a rotary-dial pay phone with an old Ma Bell logo above it. There's even a whole garden of plants in the window, though they haven't been watered in a while.

Jackie died a few years back, and her photo is above the cash register. Her husband now runs the place. No one seems to be able to locate any eight-track tapes, so when the jukebox goes unfed the place gets silent, which is probably why the word "soporific" is often used to describe it. (As in, "tending to cause sleep," or "tending to dull awareness.") But I don't see it that way. Witty rapport, honest answers, and dubious reasoning—it's all quite stimulating.

Dive Bar Rating

Jeremy's Ale House

228 Front St (Beekman Street & Peck Slip)
Transit: 2, 3, 4, 5, A, C, J, M, Z to Fulton St   *(212) 964-3537*

Currently located smack in the middle of South Street Seaport's historic district and sharing a cobblestoned block with several high-end eateries, Jeremy's Ale House started out as a concession stand catering to fisherman working on the nearby docks, but now caters to anyone looking for something grimy and unpretentious.

Dozens of autographed bras and swimsuits hang from the ceiling (supposedly there are ties too, but I didn't see any) which are said to have been donated by patrons in celebration of life milestones. Whatever emotional significance they carry, they mostly serve to randy the place up. It could use some of that, after all, as the drunks, fish mongers and gamblers who inhabit it tend to put 17-minute Pink Floyd songs on the jukebox. ("Dogs" should be stricken from internet playlists.) Beer is served in 32-ounce Styrofoam cups and 16-ounce plastic ones, the counters are topped with rolls of paper towels and the menu is filled with all sorts of fried seafood shit. You can get non-seafood items as well, such as onion rings (very nice) and cheeseburgers (not so much). When your food is ready, they'll call out your order at the top of their lungs.

It wasn't too long ago that Jeremy's moved into its current digs—the place has moved at least twice over the years—which include both an oddly-shaped pentagonal main room and an equally-odd pentagonal men's room. But it already feels lived in and gone-to-seed. The bar's mascot, which I think is a moose head, has been obscured by bras, and the tables are wobbly and lightly coated with ketchup. But it's tough not to root for the place, if only for its gritty spirit, one which clearly can not be gentrified or washed out with Formula 409.

Dive Bar Rating

Jimmy's Corner

140 W 44th St (6th Ave and 7th Ave)
Transit: 1, 2, 3, S, 7, N, Q, R, W, A, C, E to 42nd St   *(212) 221-9510*

A boxer takes a "dive" when he loses on purpose, and the word retains something of this flavor when describing bars. One accounting of the term's origin comes from the taverns frequented by young Londoners in the 19th century. Despite possessing the means to visit fancier spots, these men chose lowbrow places their fathers wouldn't have been caught dead in. This usage is slightly different from how we think of dive bars now, as dingy holes serving cheap booze to a working-class clientele.

Jimmy's Corner, then, is a dive in the old-timey English sense. It's not dirty and it's not populated by local lowlifes; its Times Square location ensures out-of-towners. But don't be afraid—these aren't your obese Wisconsinite, guidebook-lugging tourist types, but savvy businessmen seeking refuge from their philistine colleagues. Polishing off well drinks at Jimmy's long front bar or in its cramped back room, they appear to be long-distance regulars who cashed in a tip from a local.

New Yorkers would be wise to follow their own advice, as Jimmy's not only offers sanctuary from its crowded, overpriced surroundings but functions as a shrine to boxing in the Empire State. Owner Jimmy Glenn is a former pugilist himself, a one-time assistant trainer to heavyweight champ Floyd Patterson. Glenn opened the bar in 1971 to support a gym he ran, and the walls are crammed with old ringside photos and promotional posters featuring everyone from Muhammad Ali to Sugar Ray Leonard to Mike Tyson. Young champs like Floyd Mayweather Jr. are said to drop in occasionally.

However, what really sold my friend Jess and me on Jimmy's was its jukebox. Contrary to popular opinion, *Back in Black* and *Exile on Main Street* do not a great juke make. Nor do *Slippery When Wet* or Tom Petty's *Greatest Hits*. A great jukebox enhances the character a bar already possesses, which is why Nina Simone, Count Basie, Stax soul and Sinatra standards sound so right here.

Dive Bar Rating

Joe's Bar

520 E. 6th St (Avenue A and Avenue B)

Transit: L to 1st Ave   *(212) 473-9093*

When I walked into Joe's Bar, folks were singing along with "You Never Even Called Me By My Name." It was the original version, by David Allan Coe, which purports to be the "perfect country and western song." Its final verse goes:

Well, I was drunk the day my mom got out of prison
And I went to pick her up in the rain
But before I could get to the station in my pickup truck
She got runned over by a damned old train

The crowd in the bar was a seriously diverse crew of rabble rousers, including a tattooed Japanese girl in a sequined belt, a Lil Wayne-lookalike wearing a winter cap balanced atop his dreadlocks, and a leopard-print clad cougar at the bar. There was even a guy in a suit and tie, mingling near the pool table.

Joe's is falling apart, but very slowly, and it's fun to examine its various nooks and crannies, each in a different stage of decay. There's an empty storage locker in the back, a blown-up Elvis stamp (the young version), and a giant, Soviet-era Lowenbrau clock.

At one point, Lil Wayne Lookalike put down his pool cue and walked over to the jukebox. Shortly afterwards Steve Earle came on, and then Merle Haggard. I may have been drunk, but it seemed as if Lil Wayne Lookalike was responsible for keeping the cowboy hat music going. You know, someone should really write the perfect country and western song about Joe's Bar.

Dive Bar Rating

BUCK HUNTER OR BIG BUCK SAFARI

Turkey's Nest Tavern

Bushwick Country Club

Vazac's Horseshoe Bar / 7B

Sophie's

Lazy Catfish

The Blue Donkey Bar

Subway Inn

Joe's Bar & Grill

257 Avenue U

Transit: F to Avenue U (718) 372-9595

Dive Bar Ben was out of hand by the time we got to Joe's Bar & Grill. About six drinks and six bummed cigarettes into our tour of Bensonhurst dives, my chubby, unshaven, philosophical friend was loudly complaining about his ex-girlfriend Angelika, who, if you recall from the review of the Homestretch Pub, was trying to make sure he never saw their yet-unborn child. Why? Ben wasn't sure, but suspected another ex-boyfriend was involved.

At Joe's Bar & Grill, he borrowed a dollar from me and put the Stones' "Angie" on the jukebox, proceeding to sing along *as loudly as he could.* The sing hit close to home, he explained to astonished bartender Fran, who would have seen it all by now, I thought. This was near the end of the night; earlier Ben been arguing with the various Italian-American bar flies—all standing, all Republicans—about the merits of Obama's health care plan. Eventually he won them over, however, by discoursing at length on Frank Zappa, The Who and The Allman Brothers. "Zappa was a badass," he said, to nods.

Joe's Bar & Grill, not to be confused with Joe's Bar in the East Village, is a dark, intimidating place; the lights are kept low and the clientele is rowdy. "He's my brother!" a guy in a wife beater said of a guy with a shaved head who was hugging him aggressively in a violent show of heterosexual emotion. "I'll go to the mat for that guy!" Somebody's dry cleaning hung on the basement door; a neon-green sign promised jell-o shots at Mindy's 50th birthday party; the Off-Track-Betting channel played on TV.

But the place has got all sorts of neat details, like the deco, pastel-tiled floor, which is as old as the bar itself, about seventy-five or so. There are also photo montages near the back, featuring shots of deceased former regulars and Pope John Paul II. Rosaries hang from thumb tacks there, as they do from a mini wine-cask behind the bar. Italian, Irish and American flags fly out front.

After Ben sang "Shattered" at the top of his lungs it was clearly time to go, and for him to face the reality of his life. But when we got outside all he wanted to do was bum more cigarettes and talk about how many political rallies he'd been arrested at (26) and how many bars in the East Village he'd been 86'ed from (all of them). And, of course, he wanted to discuss Zappa. "How did he die?" I inquired, wondering if the "Don't Eat The Yellow Snow" hedonist was the best role model for a guy who looked like a walking heart attack. "Prostate cancer," Ben said, "which is fitting because he had such giant balls."

Dive Bar Rating 🍾🍾🍾🍾🍾

John Street Bar & Grill

17 John Street, Basement (Broadway and Nassau St)

Transit: 2, 3, 4, 5, A, C, J, M, Z Fulton St-Broadway-Nassau   *(212) 349-4659*

An evening at the John Street Bar & Grill feels like a frat party at a poorly maintained, off-campus house. You know, the one belonging to that chapter that was kicked off campus for medieval hazing practices involving horses.

Like at all bars in the financial district, the scene at this low-lit, underground cavern is in full swing by 6:30 p.m. during the week. But it's clear that nobody here is making the big Wall Street money. They're grunts, more like, and they're packed in accordingly. Surely one of the biggest drinkeries in the city, John Street can hold hundreds of folks, and that's not even including the dining area, which some use to play flip cup rather than dine.

Regarding the food itself, I stayed away based on a conversation I heard between two coked up guys in the bathroom. One was wearing a turban, and both were snorting water off of their fingertips to activate those last little bits of powder in their nose membranes. "What did you think of the nachos?" asked one. "Could've been a lot better," said the other. Other than that, the bar has a fairly standard list of adult toys—dart boards, pool table, TVs around every turn. It's differentiated from typical cattle calls in the area by two things. The first are the drink specials, like the Thursday happy hour offering all the beer you can drink for ten dollars. The second is the smoking policy, which is roughly this: You step outside the bar and smoke in the hallway. No one bothers themselves to actually walk up the stairs and go outside. I believe this is illegal, because at a nearby underground pub called Suspenders they have basically the same set-up, except in the hallway they also have a sign that says, "No smoking. Please go outside. Sorry, it's the law."

Dive Bar Rating

WEST VILLAGE, MANHATTAN

NEW YORK CITY'S BEST DIVE BARS

With its iconic neon "Bar" sign and cozy atmosphere, Johnny's possesses a carefree, throwback character in an area that's increasingly less-so. Across the street, for example, you'll find a typical West Village new-construction monstrosity: an expensive gym with giant windows, the type favored by women—and men—who love to be gawked at while working on their gluts.

Johnny's is full of gregarious people. Hell, the now-married publishers of this book initiated a one-night stand here, capping off their relationship. It's hard not to get to know your fellow tipplers, after all, since the space is so small. A row of stools lining the wall are almost impossible to sit in without getting brushed (or lightly groped) by passersby heading towards the ridonkulously-tiny rest rooms in the back. Women should be prepared to ask the bartender for toilet paper.

The shot of the day—a rotation of cheekily-named concoctions like Shit on the Grass, Citron my Face, Dirty Girl Scout Cookie and Witch's Clit—will run you $3.50. As indicated by the titles of these elixirs, Johnny's is almost too clever for its own good, and, with its license plates, foreign currency and other knick knacks on the walls, the décor style could be characterized as "Dive Bar Chic." In fact, the place feels more like a museum paying tribute to a dive bar than an actual dive bar. You're unlikely to see much in the way of working class folks here, for example. But, in a neighborhood better known nowadays for Magnolia's cupcakes than as a purveyor of counterculture, Johnny's cheap drinks and lack of pretense qualify it as a boozy oasis.

Dive Bar Rating

Julius

159 West 10th St (Waverly Place)

Transit: 1 to Christopher St; A, C, E, B, D, F, M to 4th St   *(212) 929-9672*

Reportedly a favorite of Tennessee Williams, Truman Capote and Rudolf Nureyev, Julius is New York's oldest gay bar and was the site of a "sip-in" in 1966. At the time, the State Liquor Board regulated against serving homosexuals in bars, but three men decided to challenge the mandate by walking into Julius, announcing their orientation and asking to be served. They weren't, and a photograph of the bartender placing his hand over their drinks helped spark a movement to stop gay persecution and police entrapment, paving the way for the opening of the nearby Stonewall Inn a year later. That watering hole was the site of the 1969 Stonewall riots, a clash between patrons and police that set off the modern gay rights movement.

Julius's character nowadays is that of comfortable, historic dive, in the vein of McSorley's Old Ale House. The clientele skews toward grayhairs, and the spot is not intimidating for straight guys, as can sometimes be the case at gay bars. (At the risk of sounding homophobic, let me explain that it's not that we think we're going to be harassed, it's just that we're not used to other men being so friendly.) A rainbow flag is wound between the posts of a fence in the back room, and the bouncer sings along with Kylie Minogue and Liza Minnelli.

Featuring barrel seats and tables, wagon wheel chandeliers, a propped-open door and a long, roomy interior, Julius is relaxing and usually quiet enough to permit conversation. About the only thing unpleasant about the place is the constant, overpowering smell of grease and hamburgers. There's also a leaky urinal and standing water in the bathroom. But if you can't handle the smell of grease and standing water, you probably shouldn't be consulting a book about dive bars.

Dive Bar Rating

Kevin Barry's

56 Willoughby Street and 140 Lawrence Street

Transit: A, C, F Jay St. / Borough Hall (718) 488-8901

Kevin Barry's has two wings. One is a bar/eatery with an entrance on Willoughby that is usually only open Mondays through Fridays. The other is more of a lounge/nightspot with an entrance on Lawrence Street. You can get food on either side, and they have various specials involving dinner and drink combinations; one ingenious offer slices a dollar off of your lunch bill for every beer that you order.

Before arriving with an empty stomach, however, keep in mind that the owners of the place don't seem very familiar with the health code. From 2006 through 2009, Kevin Barry's received over 90 violation points with the NYC Department of Health and Mental Hygiene for transgressions such as spoiled food, toilets not maintained, improper hand washing facility and open bait stations. That last was probably a good idea, however, considering the size of the vermin in these parts. To wit: Shortly after departing the Lawrence Street exit on a Saturday night, Anna and I saw and heard rustlings in a series of garbage bags just steps from the door. A dozen large rats proceeded to emerge from the bags, one after another, fleeing for the gutters like they were being called by the pied piper. In the bar's defense, a large construction site on Willoughby may have been partly responsible for providing the rodents' harbor.

If you're still reading this review, Kevin Barry's is actually a decent place to get a drink and your groove on. Their Saturday night party would certainly make *Onion* columnist Smoove B proud. The music is New Jack Swing and other varieties of '90s R&B, and the patrons have the earrings, hairdos and dresses to match. It's a sexy place if you're in the mood, what with the red walls, mood lighting and BlackStreet jams. There's even a VIP section, though it only consists of one booth and doesn't offer much privacy. Just be sure to watch where you step while you're doing your stepping.

Dive Bar Rating

Lazy Catfish

593 Lorimer St (Conselyea Street & Metropolitan Avenue)
Transit: L, G to Lorimer St   *(718) 599-9055*

Though Lazy Catfish is clearly a dive bar, it somehow thinks it's a bistro. It's the only place in town where you'll find linoleum on the floor and $9.50 fried red tomatoes on the menu, duct-taped vinyl benches and $11.50 chicken pot pies. Nouveau south cuisine is on offer, which is odd for a spot that also has weekly happy hours with free cans of PBR, and Big Buck Safari in the back room.

Not surprisingly, the crowd's a weird mix of white-haired immigrants, earthy types, black guys, sports fans and gentrifiers who came for the pan-fried Cajun catfish. There's not a lot of co-mingling, which seems a propos for this stretch of Williamsburg.

Peeking through the window of a storage room in the basement gives an idea of Lazy Catfish's many identity crises over the years. There's an expansive—but mostly empty—wine rack, a dusty turntable and a box containing an electronic dartboard. One wishes the joint would simply embrace its identity as a dive. For inspiration, it need only look down the block to Jr & Son, at the corner of Lorimer and Metropolitan, which is a truly grimy dive bar, one where it feels like bad things will happen to you when you walk in. (Indeed, a commenter on Time Out New York's site warns: "For the love of god, do not go into this bar.") I went twice; the first time they were closing early as I arrived. "The bartender got sick," said the guy turning off the lights. "It's been a rough day." I tried again a few weeks later but they were closed again for no discernable reason. So I can't really recommend Jr & Son, but from my brief peek inside it had clearly embraced its destiny as a glorious hellhole. Lazy Catfish should do the same.

Dive Bar Rating

Lit Lounge

93 2nd Ave (5th St and 6th St) *www.litloungenyc.com*

Transit: 6 to Astor Place; F,V to 2nd Ave; R to 8th St *(212) 777-7987*

Lit Lounge purports to promote "de-gentrification" and "un-steril-ized anti-chic." That's a fancy way of saying it's a dive bar, I guess.

Actually, Lit Lounge doubles as an art gallery and triples as a concert space. The gallery is in the back and showcases the work of "underrepresented" artists. When I was there, the walls were cov-ered by large sheets of cursive scribbles, which were actually an epic love poem written by artist Jack Walls, the long-time boyfriend of photographer Robert Mapplethorpe. (There were also photos of the two of them having sex. At least I think it was the two of them.) The rock venue is in the basement, and has low ceilings and exposed pipes. Bring earplugs, because the acoustics are terrible. The space is hard to find—your best bet is to follow the "exit" signs. The main bar doesn't have a sign out front either, so just look for number 93 and some notices warning you to watch for pickpockets and not to leave your belongings unattended.

The mysteriousness is part of what makes Lit Lounge fun; it's like entering a secret club. You descend a few steps from the street and then, pow, you're in a dark room with the Talking Heads' "Psy-cho Killer" playing at ninety-five decibels. The mirror behind the bar is covered with stickers and dollar bills, and the entire space walks a line between "premeditated arty" and "gone to seed." It's only been open since 2002, though, so the former influence is still stronger than the latter. If you look closely you'll notice carefully designed touches like small pink lights running along the walls.

Lit Lounge's heart is in the right place. It wants to be bad, it's just trying to figure out exactly how that's done.

Dive Bar Rating

Manitoba's

99 Avenue B (6th St & 7th St)   *www.manitobas.com*
Transit: L to 1st Ave   *(212) 982-2511*

Manitoba's proprietor, "Handsome Dick" Manitoba, started out as the roadie for seminal NYC punk group The Dictators, eventually graduating to singing lead vocals for the band. They are credited as the first in their genre to release a major label album, 1975's *The Dictators Go Girl Crazy!* In photos from this era—which are hung all around his bar—Dick sports a giant Jew-fro and rubs elbows with folks like Muddy Waters and the Ramones.

Nowadays he's usually seen in a knit Yankees' cap, and his primary gigs are singing with Detroit group MC5, hosting a radio show on Steven Van Zandt's satellite radio channel and, of course, bar ownership. Well over a decade old, it's fair to say that Manitoba's has been nearly as successful as The Dictators. The place is a comfy spot that features a painting of a firm-buttocks-ed nude male diving into a lake on one of the bathroom doors. It also offers *true* happy hours—chopping the price of just about everything in half—and air hockey and table hockey in the basement. (You know, table hockey. That USA vs. USSR thing, under a dome.)

Though old Dodgers and Yankees pictures cover a busted-up mirror in the back, the place is almost too sparkling to be a proper dive. But it maintains its punk rock mentality; the "secret" bathroom in the basement is said to be a favorite snogging spot when it's open. Also, the bartenders tend to be of the rock-lifer variety. Mine boasted pectoral-length, wet curly hair and wore a shirt advertising a band called Valient Thorr, who have albums called *Total Universe Man* and *Legend of the World.* Behind the bar, they've got Dick's book for sale, *The Official Punk Rock Book of Lists*, as well as "I Heart Dick" t-shirts. No doubt.

Dive Bar Rating

EAST VILLAGE, MANHATTAN

NEW YORK CITY'S BEST DIVE BARS

Mars Bar

25 East 1st St (2nd St & Extra Place)

Transit: F, M to 2nd Ave; 6 to Bleecker St   *(212) 473-9842*

Nearly every square inch of Mars Bar is covered with tags and hastily-crafted pieces of profane art, including a vagina close-up painted in watercolor. Not far from that someone has written on the wall: "Lauren (Hearts) Scott," except that "Scott" has been crossed out and "DOG RAPE" written in its place.

One time when I was there, a doughy, beaten-down dude pulled a surely-stolen leather purse from a plastic bag and told a twenty-something girl sitting nearby that he was "taking a survey." She wasn't impressed by his wares. "But if it was your style, would you like it?" he pleaded. My friend Kevin, meanwhile, asked the bartender what kind of beer they had. She didn't say anything, but simply gestured to the row of cases stacked behind the bar: Coors Light, Yuengling, Dos Equix, Corona.

Hot, dark and small, Mars Bar is *the* quintessential New York dive bar. The front door is unmarked, but you're in the right place if there are homeless guys out front. (They rotate in and out, occasionally attempting to smoke inside, with varying degrees of success.) There's a long bar, stools, a jukebox, and that's about it. The small, square windows at the front seem to indicate that it used to be an auto body shop, although the bartender speculated that it was once a Catholic Worker food kitchen. There's no background music unless someone puts on some Barry White or Flamingos. This means you get snippets of conversations, like the guy talking about how he tried to cook blueberry muffins using his broiler. Or the girl recalling the time gutter punks stood on the bar singing Hank Williams, and frat boys began hurling shot glasses at each other. One of them hit a gutter punk's head and ricocheted off, shattering a bottle of vodka. A brawl followed.

Everyone has a Mars Bar story. My story is about the time I was there and it was pitch black. It was so dark I couldn't see my beer. Finally a patron climbed atop the bar and twisted a bare bulb, and no one even seemed to notice. My Mars Bar story may not be as good as other people's, but it's true.

Dive Bar Rating

McSorley's Old Ale House

15 East 7th Street (Cooper Square & Taras Shevchenko Place)

Transit: 6 to Astor Place; R to 8th St   *(212) 473-9148*

In *Low Life*, his classic chronicle of old New York debauchery and corruption, author Luc Sante describes the average late nineteenth century Bowery saloon. The place had a sawdust-covered floor and walls covered with newspaper clippings, mirrors, nudes and chromolithographs of boxers and horses. In some spots a "stein of beer was drawn and dumped in front of you the minute you sat down," while others would not allow females in, "even to fill a growler with take-out beer, making them wait on the sidewalk in front."

Sound like fun? Well that's exactly what you'll still find at McSorley's Old Ale House, although the courts forced them to open their doors to the fairer sex in 1970. A celebration of old-timey conspicuous consumption (of beer), it's the kind of place that makes screaming at the top of your lungs seem like perfectly acceptable indoor behavior, the kind of place where you'll leave with suds all over your jacket without knowing how they got there.

Established in 1854 and said to be the oldest American bar in continuous operation, you can smell McSorley's from a half block away; the stench comes from the floor, which is a disgusting mess of sawdust, beer and dirty napkins. The bar is also famous for withholding creature comforts. Thus, there are no stools, nothing alcoholic except for their two beers—a sweet-tasting lager and an ale—and usually, little to no room.

Drinking chants and general screaming will interrupt your conversation, so it's better not to talk and simply watch the 'tendars (as they call each other) in action. The steady stream of traffic and small serving sizes require them to almost always be filling or cleaning mugs. The latter process only takes about three seconds; with eight mugs in each hand, they'll pass them through soapy water in one motion and then rinse them in the next. Beers will run you $4.50 each for two medium-sized mugs, which might seem like a great deal until the foam dies down and you're left with barely more than half a glass of beer. If you pay with a big bill, the 'tendars will dump your change on the sopping wet counter, so you'll have no choice but to leave a big tip.

With layers of bric-a-brac on the walls, McSorley's is full of memorabilia, from JFK shrines and portraits of Babe Ruth to campaign buttons and rifles. Perhaps the most interesting bits are the dust-encrusted, dangling wishbones in the back. As the story goes, soldiers set to depart for World War I would hang them above the bar after a meal, in the hopes that they would survive to one day come back and retrieve them. If they did, they would take their bone down and have a drink for those who were not so lucky. Like many old bar stories, this one is perhaps apocryphal, but that doesn't necessarily make it any less touching.

Dive Bar Rating

McSwiggan's Bar

393 2nd Ave (22nd St & 23rd St)

Transit: 6 to 23rd St　　　　　　　　　　　　　　*(212) 683-3180*

This "Swiggiest place on earth!" seems to mock the tradition of Irish Pubs in America, to its credit. The term "Irish Pub" is redundant, after all, and like most of them, McSwiggan's Bar is about as Irish as my cat Nora. To be fair, perhaps some of the NYU students who come in have attempted to read *Finnegans Wake* (which you should not do, by the way, as the professor of a Ulysses course I once took admitted to barely being able to understand *Finnegans Wake*, even with the help of a study group composed of other Joyce scholars).

McSwiggan's has been cleaned up a bit in recent times, and its neon green "Bar" sign probably beckons to collegians who normally wouldn't dive. That's a shame, because it'd be nice to have McSwiggan's in your back pocket as that quiet bar to bring your significant other to. Soft red lights illuminate the bottles of booze. The premises are dark enough to permit snuggling up, but the dart board has its own lighting system to accommodate the loners who throw missiles in the afternoon by themselves. (Note: Activating said system requires asking the bartender, who wears one of those oval-shaped knit caps—swollen to hold all of her hair—for assistance.)

Other patrons who haunt the premises before the young geniuses arrive include nurses wearing scrubs, dodgy dudes in thick winter jackets who order two bottles of Bud and drink them alone near the pool table and guys sipping milky cocktails who argue with their girlfriends on their cell phones. McSwiggan's appeal lies partly in its sixteen beers on tap and a wide selection of liquors, but it get bonus points for playing that Killers song that doesn't make any sense. "And I'm on my knees looking for the answer," it goes. "Are we human or are we dancer?"

Dive Bar Rating

GREAT JUKEBOXES

Jimmy's Corner

Vazac's Horseshoe Bar / 7B

Joe's Bar

Mars Bar

Doc Holliday's

Milady's Bar & Restaurant

160 Prince St (Broadway & Thompson)

Transit: C,E to Spring St;R to Prince St; 1 to Houston   *(212) 226-9340*

Why are we obsessed with camp? No, not those tent-filled spots in the woods, but rather the nostalgic, often-pastel cultural bits that decorate fabulous homes and eateries around the country. While you'll have to read Susan Sontag's essay "Notes On 'Camp'" for a thorough answer to this question, it's clear that camp is a defining characteristic of dive bars.

Some dives are camp without realizing it—those Christmas lights were intended to fancy the place up, don'tcha know—while others purposely celebrate the tacky side of life. Dubiously-decorated spots catering to older patrons like East Harlem's Puerto Rico-USA Bar fall in the former category, while ironic, hipster-oriented bars like Welcome To The Johnson's on the Lower East Side fall into the latter.

Milady's Bar & Restaurant is somewhere in the middle. Its linoleum floors, plastic red ketchup bottles and utilitarian diner-style tables suggest a place that's fallen from fashion, but its pink neon sign above the bar and jukebox—which contains both Patsy Cline and Digital Underground—imply a spot with its tongue firmly planted in its cheek. Fittingly, the place draws a diverse crowd, from faux-hawked, hairy-pitted lesbians to guys in Mets' jerseys playing pool. Regulars tend to read whatever they want into the polka-dotted marquee above the front door.

Newcomers tend not to realize that Milady's is also a restaurant, which is why a busboy, playing host, intercepts you the minute your feet leave the flattened beer box that serves as a door mat, guiding you to your preferred section of the establishment, the bar or the eatery, which are separated by a shoulder-high eyesore of a divider. If you're at all hungry, you'd be advised to try the food. I would suggest either the tater tots or the chicken wings, which, for $6.99 are very generously proportioned and come with an equally-generous side of celery. There's nothing at all ironic about that.

Dive Bar Rating

Milano's Bar

51 E Houston St (Mulberry Street & Mott Street)

Transit: B, D, F, M to Broadway-Lafayette; 6 to Bleeker St   *(212) 226-8844*

The Nolita dive bar experience can be had both at Milano's Bar and, just steps away, Botanica Bar. They're both dark and worn down. But Milano's contains middle-aged adults who call each other "darling" and "gorgeous" before imploring their fellow patrons to "get the fuck out of here and get home to your kids." Botanica, on the other had, offers twenty-somethings wearing "Free Gaza" t-shirts and punching on their iPhones. Milano's soundtrack is Grateful Dead, Elton John and oldies, while Botanica's music comes courtesy of bands you've never heard before. Different strokes for different folks.

In a city full of skinny pubs, Milano's is perhaps the narrowest, stretching to only about nine feet at its widest point. The place is so small that the only storage space must be accessed through a portal in the sidewalk, which means that once the vermouth is gone so is the barkeep, at least for a few minutes. Not surprisingly, everybody is into each other's business, which is a hallmark of a good dive bar, as are $3 Miller Lite pints and mass singalongs when The Four Seasons' "Sherry Baby" comes on the jukebox.

The bar is crammed to the rafters with nostalgia for old New York, from the saloon-style doors to the portraits of Sinatra, Marilyn, Chaplin, the Yankees and hundreds of sloshed patrons lining the walls. Though the joint's name implies Italian ownership, legend has it that an Irishman won it in a drinking match. (Well, Yelp.com commenter Katie M has it, anyway.) If true, it wasn't a bad haul. So long as he wasn't claustrophobic.

Dive Bar Rating

Mona's

My friend Matt is a classically-trained pianist who sometimes sits in on Mona's weekly jazz sessions. The last time he'd gone the bar's piano had barely functioned, he told me when we went there recently, so he was psyched to see that they'd replaced it. But after a quick test run he found that the new one was scratched up and also played poorly. "It was probably donated from somebody's basement," he speculated.

Despite its less-than-perfect percussion, Mona's continues to draw Matt due to its ultra-relaxed vibe. It is low lit and cavernous, with a banged-up pool table and a small room way in the back with nothing but a foosball table and a red neon Guinness sign. The furniture is a mishmash of vinyl booths, wooden benches and random chairs, with the occasional blue-stained glass lantern hanging overhead. When the music isn't live—they also do Irish jam sessions from time to time—it's mainly Beach Boys, Springsteen or Roy Orbison. Presiding over the scene is Mona herself, and it's hard not to fall for her bright-red, boisterously curly hair and Irish brogue. (I assume it's Irish, in any case. I'm horrible at identifying accents.)

A Guinness costs $3 all day on Thursdays, and cigarettes can often be had for a discount, too. That is, so long as the self-dubbed "cigarette man" is on the premises; you'll know him by the $7 packs he dispenses from his duffel bag. He's got a pretty brazen sales pitch, but he knows nobody is going to hassle him at Mona's, as folks here tend not to be prone to bellyaching. That is, other than about the inferior quality of the piano.

Dive Bar Rating

Montero's Bar & Grill

73 Atlantic Ave (Hicks Street)

Transit: 2, 3, 4, 5, M, R, W to Court St-Borough Hall   *(718) 624-9799*

The building of the BQE pushed Montero's Bar & Grill out of its original haunt far down Atlantic Avenue near the East River, with the current incarnation opening across the street in 1947 when owner Joseph Montero dropped a $1000 down payment on the location. The pub originally catered to sailors, longshoremen, and others employed by nearby piers 5, 6 and 7, but now it mainly serves a rapidly-gentrifying community. It remains, however, crammed from floor to ceiling with shipping ephemera, memorabilia and knick knacks, including life rafts that literally hang in your face.

The bar's history and nostalgia ensure its favored status among writers, who have probably spilled more ink on it than any New York dive besides McSorley's. (It doesn't hurt that Montero's BoCo-Ca neighborhood is home to more scribes than you can shake a dead squid at.) Times writers seem particularly enamored of it, routinely penning 2500 word screeds without breaking a sweat, with titles like "My Brooklyn; A Raffish Reminder, Landlubbers, of Saltier Days."

That isn't to say that Montero's isn't wonderful. Indeed, with its wooden telephone booths, ships in bottles and wall-mounted displays showcasing old-timey locals and their dogs, it's downright charming. It's just…what more is there to say about it? The Monteros once bragged about hiring "young girls with nice legs," but my barkeep was a crusty middle-aged guy in a t-shirt who scampered outside for frequent smoke breaks. I quite liked him, actually; unlike most bartenders, who leave your dollar tips alone until you depart, he snatched them up immediately after they were set down on the bar.

Dive Bar Rating

Motor City Bar

127 Ludlow St (Delancey St & Rivington St)

Transit: F, J, M, Z to Delancey-Essex; 2nd Ave to F, M   *(212) 358-1595*

The owners of Motor City probably hired a decorating consultant to create the grimy image they were going for. For example, while the place is dark and seedy, it seems to be intentionally dark and seedy. Similarly, if you look carefully, the graffiti on the walls is just a little too tidy, and the aged-looking signs and other Michigan ephemera are actually reproductions. The bottle opener hanging on a coiled cord from the ceiling and the "Welcome to Detroit, the Renaissance City" sign are also just a little too perfect as well. And come on, what kind of dive has fancy candles sitting at each table?

Despite the dive-y façade, however, if you're looking for an unpretentious place with an edge on the Lower East Side, Motor City Bar is a damn fine choice. As much as I hate to admit it, the interior decorator knew what he or she was doing. The no-frills black and red vinyl seats are sleek and comfortable, the punk rock is ferocious and the space is huge, big enough to permit one to find a seat on a Saturday night and big enough that long-haired skaters are able to pull their boards from their bags and ride them to the bar.

In a way, Motor City is a perfect representation of the Lower East Side's schizophrenic character, a somewhat awkward attempt to reconcile the neighborhood's rowdy past with its commercial present. But if the moneyed pigs are going to invest their money on relaxed, easy spaces where a pint only costs five bucks and Detroit Red Wing towels hang from behind the bar, I say cheers to capitalist swine.

Dive Bar Rating

BEST NAMES

Alibi

Beer Goggles

Distinguished Wakamba Cocktail Lounge

Golden Cicada Tavern

Irish Eyes

Jackie's 5th Amendment

Mr. McGoo's

Mr. McGoo's

5602 Broadway (West 231st St and West 232nd St

Transit: 1 to 231st St   *718-548-9810*

Lots of wise guys hang out at Mr. McGoo's, and I mean that mostly in the sense that they're funny guys. That said, almost all of them are overweight, have mustaches or talk like Joe Pesci. A night there might go something like this:

Fat guy #1: You like my sauce?

Bald guy: I told you I like your sauce.

Fat guy #1: No, you said you had a toothache that night.

Fat guy #2: (Talking on phone) I love you and I don't even know your name. What's your name?

Bartender: (To me and my friend Rose) 500 pounds of fun.

Fat guy #2: Delilah? (Pauses) I'm not big on names. (Pauses) I'm telling you, don't let him use your hairspray. (Hangs up phone. To bald guy) You guys gotta come skiing with us. Hunter Mountain. Last year, I was drunk 71 out of 72 hours, and the other hour I was passed out, so I may have been drunk then, too, I just don't remember. They treat me like a king up there. And the food! We get up, wave hello at the slopes and then go get drunk. Although I went tubing last time.

Bald guy: How many times?

Fat guy #2: Four times.

Bald guy: Four times?

Fat guy #2: They didn't tell me that the fatter you are, the faster you go. It was terrifying. Me and this other guy tied our tubes together and went down the hill at 850 miles an hour.

Bald guy: (To me and Rose) That's 850 miles an hour, remember, not 856.

Bartender: (To me and Rose) You guys should come.

Fat guy #1: Anybody who spends time in my summer house ain't comin' back.

Me and Rose: See you guys later.

Dive Bar Rating

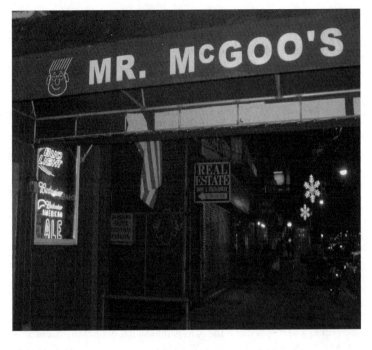

Nancy Whiskey Pub

1 Lispenard St (Ave Of The Americas & West Broadway)

Transit: A, C, E to Canal St; J, M, Z, N, Q, R, W, 6 to Canal   *(212) 226-9943*

At the best dive bars, the misery and dread is balanced by elation and poorly-reasoned optimism. Rot and decay hang in the air, but so does self-affirmation. The patrons and the help relate to each other like dysfunctional family members, bitter and defiant one moment, gentle and supportive the next.

The popular, bushy-bearded bartender at Nancy Whiskey Pub is known as The Pirate, both for his manner of speaking and because he is said to have once wore an eye patch. (I have no idea if that last bit is true.) He tends to accommodate his customers, unlike the younger, female, brunette barkeep, who does things to annoy the aging clientele, like blasting Arcade Fire at ear-splitting levels. When one of the old-timers requested that she switch the big television to the U.S. Open so he that could watch the women's quarterfinals, she refused, claiming that she was watching the soccer game on the screen, though when pressed, she couldn't name either of the teams that were playing. Not that the old timer knew much about tennis himself, continuing to insist that the seventeen-year-old from Georgia was "making her move" right up to the end of her 6-2, 6-2 loss.

Nancy Whiskey Pub's employees and customers probably get on each other's nerves because the place stinks so badly of cheap French fry oil. Maybe they're worried they'll be burned up, what with the kitchen's greasy grill continually spawning foot-high flames. The ceiling is extremely low in many parts of the bar—at six feet, I can't stand in the upstairs loft— and every inch is cluttered. Stacks of cardboard beer cases and a shuffleboard table dominate the main floor; one suspects the table's main function is to provide storage below for yet more cases of beer.

Yet Nancy's charm is somehow enough to serve as the Gorilla Glue bonding its inhabitants together. Maybe it's the cheap drinks, or the "Fuck Communism" house t-shirts worn by the cook and the occasional customer. Or maybe it's the simple revelation that, as ugly as things may be in here, they're down right disfigured outside.

Dive Bar Rating

Nassau Bar

118 Nassau Street (Beekman St. and Ann St.)
Transit: 2, 3, 4, 5, A, C, J, M, Z to Fulton St-Broadway-Nassau *(212) 962-0011*

Only a couple of square inches of fabric separate the Nassau Bar from being a strip club, as the bikini clad waitresses work on one side of the bar and the men stand and drink in groups on the other. Not surprisingly, the atmosphere is one of raging testosterone, with walls decorated entirely by beer signs, lounging beer models and the occasional Mets' pennant. Red Christmas lights and red bulbs dimly illuminate the room. The bathroom is gross and so small that you can't wash your hands without turning on the dryer. When I ordered a $3 can of Miller Lite, the bartender gave me a glass to go along with it, but didn't actually pour the beer in it for me. She did, however, pick up my glass and set a coaster under it, because God forbid a bit of moisture compromise the faux-wood linoleum bar.

The place shifts into high gear around 6:30 pm. By that time, it's packed to the gills with tied-and-slacksed Wall Street dudes—there wasn't a single female patron when I visited. A short, tattooed, Hobbit-like owner/manager type ran around fixing things and keeping the place in order. (God only knows what was going on behind the scenes.) I chatted up a young and stunning black bartender, who wore a pink bikini emblazoned with a skull and crossbones and had her left arm in a cast. "How'd you clip your wing?" I asked, or something to that effect. "I fell," she said, adding: "I'm just that clumsy." I couldn't tell if that was her idea of a joke. Drinks here are almost as expensive as in a strip club, and happy hour ends impossibly early, so it's best just to stick with the specials.

Dive Bar Rating

Navy Yard Cocktail Lounge

200 Flushing Ave (at Washington Ave)

Transit: G to Clinton-Washington Ave   *No phone*

Though it's often referred to as the "scariest bar in Brooklyn" and its men's toilet wears a bumper sticker for a funeral home, you should give Navy Yard Cocktail Lounge a chance.

There are friendly ladies here, after all, scantily-clad ladies who perform lap dances for drinks and tips. (Apparently, sometimes they'll do even more—the venue's proprietor admits to having been arrested for "backroom action.") One of these women, a not unattractive, soft-spoken black lady named Mystique, doubles as the bartender, and after I sat down and started scribbling in my notebook she ripped it from my hand and started reading my notes.

Half dozen small security TVs near the front door

Water-stained ceiling

Signs on 'Ladies Room' door read: 'Surveillance Cameras In Use' and '5 Minute Limit.'

"That's not very flattering," she said.

"What would you prefer I say?"

"That it's a friendly place. That everybody has a good time here."

I might be willing to sign on to that. Located on the wrong side of the BQE, across the street from the Navy Yard ("We used to launch ships. Now we launch businesses") the NYCL is a congenial place, populated by black and Latin guys playing pool and (when I was there) dancers drinking Hypnotiq and playing video poker.

Still, it's an odd place. A creepy blacklight shines from above, a (reportedly decommissioned) stripper's stage sits across from the bar, and while I was there a bearded white guy came in carrying a cardboard box of assorted liquor bottles. Mystique talked with him for a minute and then removed the jugs one at a time. One was Jack Daniels and another was the biggest container of Hennesscy I'd ever seen. I then went to the john, and when I came back Mystique had placed a metal funnel into one of the bottles she had just received and was pouring an unmarked liquid into it.

"What are you making there, Mystique?" someone asked.

"My death potion," she replied.

So, you might not feel completely comfortable here. But the building that houses Navy Yard Cocktail Lounge is for sale, and if they close it down and you've never been, you'll be sorry. Trust me.

Dive Bar Rating

O'Connor's Bar

39 5th Ave (Bergen Street and Dean Street)

Transit: 2, 3, 4, 5, M, N, Q, W, R, B, D to Atlantic Ave- Pacific St   *(718) 783-9721*

If your task was to create the first bartender, how would you design him? (Keep in mind that the first female bartender would be created later, from his rib.)

Surely his appearance would be vaguely rockabilly, to indicate his class, admiration for the old ways of doing things and a lurking wildness. He would have slicked-back hair and wear sturdy, workman jeans with a giant set of keys dangling from the belt loop. His outfit would be topped off by a wife-beater and pristine-white cowboy snap shirt, one with the sleeves rolled up to display his bicep tattoos.

He would make vodka collinses and whiskey sours in pint glasses, squeezing fresh lemons over a strainer and using real sugar, the same way his Irishman octogenarian predecessor Charlie Campbell did it before he retired a couple of years ago. He would look you in the eyes when you arrived and salute you with his hand. And he would work at O'Connor's Bar.

O'Connor's is probably the manliest bar in New York. Sure, if you're a woman you're welcome there, but it's got a nearly-overpowering masculine vibe, a John Wayne-level of sturdiness and character. Open since 1933, it's an airy, roomy spot where you're always able to find a seat. The music isn't too loud and an American flag drapes the wall above the naugahyde booths. Yeah, there are hipsters, but the ambience overwhelms them, rather than the other way around. My friend Stefan described it as the kind of place where mafia guys go to receive orders, and I can see that, if only for the talking fish mounted behind the bar a la *The Sopranos*.

Founder Patrick O'Connor died in 2006. He hated it when people called the joint a dive. "He didn't stand here all day, every day, running a cheap dump," noted *The New York Times*. "And by the way, when his was the only place around for blocks and blocks, when the drug dealers outside outnumbered the old men on the stools, he didn't hear anybody complaining."

So, I won't call it a dive. Instead, I'll call it the Garden of Eden of intoxication. And, speaking of which, I never caught the bartender's name. Frankly I was too intimidated to ask. If I'd done that he probably would have thought I had a little crush on him, or something. And that would have been preposterous.

Dive Bar Rating

Palace Cafe

206 Nassau Ave (at Russell St)

Transit: G to Nassau   *(718) 383-9848*

"Is the Franzia for sale?" I asked the bartender at the Palace Café, who looked like he was auditioning for the Howard Stern Show and had a runny nose so bad that his upper lip was glossy bright red. He'd wiped it with his bare hand before serving us.

"What do you think?" he said.

I didn't know what to think. It sort of looked like the boxes of white, red and rose were waiting to be taken out with the trash.

"How much for a glass?"

He raised three fingers.

"Only the best here," said a guy at the end of the bar. He wore a scruffy beard and looked uncomfortable in his skin. (Earlier, as he'd watched the Mets play at their new home Citi Field he'd complained, "Sushi at the baseball stadium? Can you fucking believe that?")

"Yeah," I said, playing along, "White wine at room temperature. Delicious." The room went silent. Not that there was much noise before. Apparently this is a heavy metal bar, but many nights the jukebox is off, and tonight there was nobody else here besides the scruffy beard, the flu-prone bartender and me and my friends. It was easy, then, to hear the barkeep's concluding comment, which he muttered from beneath his mane of long, wig-textured hair. "Fucking prick."

Somehow this didn't make me squirm. The $1.50 mugs of Coors Light helped, as did the place's fallen-from-grace vibe. Palace Café was clearly once a swinging joint; an attached dining room used to house a restaurant, but now only does special events. The German-style pub is filled with stained glass windows, and wrought-iron chandeliers depict fairy-tale-like scenes. There's ornate, manicured woodwork, a grand, half moon main bar and an abandoned auxiliary bar in the corner. One gets the feeling that a few years back they just gave up on the place. The beer they serve—be it Stella or Bud—is almost always flat.

Later the bartender, who had done his best to ignore me since the Franzia kerfuffle, asked me what I was writing down. I explained this project and he began to shake his head.

"Don't put us in there."

"This isn't a dive," said the scruffy beard, staring at the television, envisioning all the assholes in the Mets' fancy new stadium eating their fancy, asshole food.

"Why do you say that?" I asked.

"This isn't a dive," he repeated.

You're welcome.

Dive Bar Rating

Parkside Lounge

317 E Houston St (Attorney Street & Avenue B)

Transit: F, J, M, Z to Delancey-Essex   *(212) 673-6270*

Sometimes, you're not wearing the right jeans for the Lower East Side. Maybe they're too tight, or maybe they're not tight enough. If that happens, head to the Parkside Lounge. Yeah, it's a hipster dive, but it's filled with slightly less self-conscious hipsters than you'll find at trendier Lower East Side spots. Parkside folks don't wear their ball caps cocked to the side like those hanging out at Orchard and Stanton, but rather straight ahead. Or backwards, like in an '80s movie.

The bands playing Parkside's back room are also different from those who play at spots like Pianos, The Living Room and Arlene's Grocery. One group I saw had a goateed and ponytailed front man. He led them in a rendition of Tom Petty's "American Girl," and then they segued seamlessly into the Gummi Bears' theme song. The next group was composed of nerdy middle-aged dudes singing about the Nixon administration and terry towels. The stage is draped by multi-colored metallic streamers and features a piano that anyone can use, so long as they don't set their coat on it. (There's a sign warning against this.) The venue never charges a cover, though the performers themselves sometimes do.

The room hosts burlesque as well, but for the most part the Parkside is a rock and roll establishment. Dinosaur Jr., Built to Spill, Pavement, and Old '97s play in the main room, and in further tribute to the thirty to fortysomething crowd, the Pac Man/ Galaga sit-down console is free. That's a hell of a thing to discover when you're drunk. Of course, I had already shoved a couple of quarters into the machine, but now I know.

Dive Bar Rating

Phil Hughes Bar & Restaurant

1682 1st Ave (87th Street & 88th Street)
Transit: 4,5,6 to 86th St (212) 722-9415

My friend Jed described Yorkville's Phil Hughes Bar & Restaurant as the type of place your deadbeat dad would go to watch the Giants game. Archetypal patrons include the surly, jean-jacket wearing old-timer giving anyone who comes into his radius menacing, drunk stares; the aging, sloppy lady drinking red wine and kissing people; and of course the guy distracted by a tin of nuts who drops his Bud bottle with a smash on the floor and proudly owns up to it. "That was me!"

Phil Hughes calls itself a "Bar & Restaurant," although, like many other fine establishments in this book, there's no evidence of an eatery. Instead, you get splintered, ripped and duct-taped chairs, air filled with cigarette smoke and the opportunity to hear "Stayin' Alive," "Night Fever," "Jive Talkin'" and "More Than A Woman" in succession. (And if you can name any more Bee Gees songs that that, you are indeed a true fan.) In a nook across from the pool table sits a light-colored piano, covered in dust and blocked in by a triumvirate of paint-splattered step-ladders. From the electrical sockets with no covers to the painting accessories stashed near the front, there's an air of neglect, as if the owner does not often come in often,

Still, Phil Hughes boasts an air of invincibility. It's spacious and made of brick, and the barkeep is strong and courteous. The joint is much older than the Yankees pitcher of the same name (for whom, contrary to rumors, it is not named) and one gets the feeling that it could survive a nuclear attack, along with the cockroaches and Eagles fans. Same difference, right?

Dive Bar Rating

Pinetree Lodge

326 E 35th St (1st Avenue & Tunnel Entrance St)

Transit: 6 to 33rd St

(212) 481-5490

There's something very calculated about the Pinetree Lodge, but damn if it takes away from the charm. It's one of those bars, like the Raccoon Lodge or Welcome to the Johnson's, that tries to recreate the atmosphere of a cozy ski chalet or somebody's den. And here, after a few drinks—the stiff happy hour cocktails come with a wooden coin good for a freebie—you kinda buy it, despite the fact that those "stacked piles" of "split firewood" are actually nubs of logs glued to the walls, and the adjacent "books" are nothing more than spines. (An actual bookshelf, meanwhile, harbors volumes from 1973's *Funk & Wagnalls New Encyclopedia*.)

The rest of the décor consists of moose heads, pelts, snowshoes, inner tubes, chandeliers made out of kindling, and red and black checkered drapes, which match the pillows on the floor. (People sit on them.) Nooks and crannies abound; eventually you'll come across the video game "Strikers 1945" and you may even be able to find the two tiny unisex bathrooms on opposite sides of the bar. Out front is a ridiculous wooden sign that reads, "Dry Goods." C'mon. What is this, *Hot Tub Time Machine*?

So, perhaps Pinetree is half whimsy and half calculation. Yes, it's a "weird" but completely nonthreatening place Murray Hill professionals can take the guys from the firm, a spot made to look ramshackle that was actually carefully designed. So what? It's still more interesting than most everything else in the neighborhood, and the food is good too. It comes courtesy of the nearby Pine Tree Lodge Bar & Grill, which has the same owners as the pub but specializes in Caribbean cuisine, of all things. I had the "Rasta Pasta." It reminded me, you know, of the old days hanging out at the ski lodge.

Dive Bar Rating

Port 41

355 W 41st St (8th Ave & 9th Ave)

Transit: A, C, E, 1, 2, 3, S, 7, N, Q, R, W to 42nd   *(212) 947-1188*

The brunette bartender, about the size and shape of Mila Kunis, says she is often asked: "Why are you wearing a bikini?" Because it's a bikini bar, she tells them. You may not know about bikini bars, but they're all over the city, filling the gaps in a metro area lacking its share of strip clubs. Though these places generally have the inflated drink prices to match, Port 41 is pretty affordable, functioning more as a sketchy dive bar than a spectacle of flesh.

The place boasts a neon "coat check" sign but no actual coat check. There is free popcorn and hot dogs, but the hot dogs are extremely grim looking. (Go to Rudy's Bar & Grill up the street if you want wieners.) When I was here, I met a long-haired, pudgy guy from Bensonhurst in a Hawaiian shirt, named Ben. He calls himself "Mr. Dive Bar" and claims to have been 86ed from dozens of dives around town. At the Grassroots Tavern, for example, he was caught smoking pot in a closet, which he says he mistook for the bathroom. He was extremely cordial, unlike the old guy with a cane who was sitting in the back room. He was watching basketball by himself, a few feet away from a totally-out-of-place wooden desk. Earlier I'd seen a young dude drop something into one of the desk drawers and now—curious type that I am—I walked over and opened the drawer.

"What are you doing?" the old guy demanded.

"Nothing," I said. "A guy put something here, and I wanted to see what it was."

"Don't worry about that!" he said.

Later, a beefy guy came into the bar carrying a large plastic bag stuffed to the gills with items I could not make out. He met up with the old guy in the back room, and later left empty handed.

Meanwhile, the bartender assured a pair of patrons that, "The top stays on."

Dive Bar Rating

DRINKS COME IN STYROFOAM
OR
PLASTIC CUPS

Greenpoint Tavern

Navy Yard Cocktail Lounge

Farrell's

Turkey's Nest

Jeremy's Ale House

Puerto Rico USA Bar

124 East 107th Street

Transit: 6 to 110th St

prusabar.com

(212) 410-1170

Puerto Rico USA Bar sits on a dilapidated Spanish Harlem block, steps away from a fenced-in lot that appears to be abandoned. The lot has a trailer, assorted furniture and other household items strewn about, and looks something like a flea market. A mailman who frequents the bar says this is not the case, however.

"People store their extra things there," explains the resident Cliff Clavin. He adds that a maintenance man lives in the trailer and operates the veritable mini-storage facility.

The arrangement is a bit odd, but many things about the Puerto Rico USA Bar are a bit odd. For example, I'd heard that while Thursdays and Fridays are "buy two drinks, get the third free" nights, tonight was salsa night. But when I walked in, the place was dead silent, save for dueling TVs. The Latin guys at the bar were watching *Law and Order*, while an old lady sitting at the dominoes table watched a telenovela.

"Isn't tonight salsa night?" I asked the bartender, a genial fella with an impeccably-kept white mustache.

"No, that's Wednesday," he said, before realizing it was Wednesday. "Ah, salsa night!" He then turned on the CD player, sending the music's euphoric strains through the air. Turns out the guy is also the owner; he grew up in the neighborhood, and Puerto Rico USA Bar has been open for about six years.

After I introduced myself and asked his name he paused, apparently convinced my Anglo tongue couldn't handle his Puerto Rican handle. "Just call me Andy," he insisted.

I asked if he could recommend anywhere nearby to eat.

"Do you want Spanish food?"

"Sure."

"There's a restaurant called La Fonda [Boricua]," he said. "Either that, or there's a KFC."

I chose the former, an excellent Puerto Rican joint without any menus where I ordered by pointing to what someone else was eating. I returned after dinner with my friend Emily, and Andy cracked mini-bottles of Schweppes for our gin and tonics, topping us off with ice whenever we needed it.

Puerto Rico USA Bar has an old clientele and a web site that is perhaps even older. Its "Photos" page features clip-art of pirates, Tom Cruise and a pixilated image of a blonde woman dumping water on her boobs. It also has unbeatable Spanglish: *Our policies is to respect one another maintaining a cool, calm and collective personality*. I couldn't have said it any better myself.

Dive Bar Rating

Raccoon Lodge

59 Warren St (West Broadway & Church Street)

Transit: 2, 3, A, C, E to Chambers-Park Pl   *(212) 227-9894*

It really is a lodge. Sort of. With six-inch slices of faux logs plating the outside, Raccoon Lodge feels apart from the city, despite being located in the financial district. Its long, semi-circular wooden bar is a work of art, and in the back nook there's a fish tank. It feels inviting today, and certainly felt that way to firefighters and Ground Zero volunteers when it reopened shortly after the 2001 attacks. For a time it was one of the only spots in the neighborhood that was open. Nowadays police and firemen gear and helmets line the walls alongside 9/11 memorials.

If it all sounds too serious, it's really not. The barkeep with the brunette ponytail and the musky voice tosses back vodka, hurls handfuls of ice at people, then comps shots for those she's pelted, to apologize. They in turn proceed to purchase massive quantities of drinks and leave her a large pile of one dollar bills. The next day the cycle repeats itself.

The suit and tie crowd know about Raccoon Lodge, and can sometimes be found here drinking Cuervo. But unlike the nearby Patriot Saloon—a corporate, wannabe dive where every hour is amateur hour—Raccoon Lodge has the occasional gamer guy with hair down to his waist to keep everybody honest. More importantly, you couldn't recreate the place's charms, as no fake dive could feel so worn in and no fake dive would hire a barkeep who gets so personal with the customers. And you can bet that no fake dive bar would have the heart to re-open its doors when the neighborhood needed it the most.

Dive Bar Rating

NEW YORK CITY'S BEST DIVE BARS

Red Hook Bait & Tackle

320 Van Brunt St (King Street & Pioneer Street) *www.redhookbaitandtackle.com*
Transit: Cab it from Carroll Street F stop *(718) 797-4892*

It's off the beaten path, yes, but if you make it to Red Hook Bait & Tackle, you also have the benefit of another excellent seedy pub, Brooklyn Ice House, next door, as well as the alpha and omega of Red Hook dives, Sunny's Bar, a half mile to the southwest.

But that's pretty much it. Red Hook is a sleepy former industrial neighborhood, and this section of Van Brunt Street has little more than bodegas, pizza joints and teenagers walking around with nothing to do. It can get so sleepy that, when I was at Red Hook Bait & Tackle on a Saturday night I was the only person in the joint, save for a kissy couple in a vinyl booth in the back. (It probably doesn't help that the front door looks like it's been boarded up.) The shaggy bartender with an indeterminate European accent was playing folk and psychedelic LPs on the record player and burning incense. I entertained myself by examining the taxidermy—bass, deer, a boar, a wolf, a freaking black bear cub—and the plastic duck glued to the ceiling upside down. The rest of the décor runs from the inspired— like the sign that says, "The two happiest days in the life of a boatman: The day he buys it and the day he sells it"—to the extremely inspired, like the Christmas-light studded mini billboard that says, simply, "Suck It."

Once in a while New Orleans-style pocket brass bands play here, whatever those are, and there are occasional burlesque shows as well. But, always, there are three dollar cans of Tecate. And even if Red Hook Bait & Tackle is quiet it's still an excellent, Lynchian outpost for when you find yourself posted on the outskirts of New York civilization.

Dive Bar Rating

Reif's Tavern

302 E 92nd St (2nd Ave and 1st Ave)
Transit: 6 to 86th St; 4,5,6 to 86th St

www.reifstavern.com
212-426-0519

Reif's Tavern has a "bring your own meat to grill" policy, which you should feel free to do when the weather is nice. (Reservations with the bartender are recommended.) You might also want to "bring your own friends," particularly if the folks you enjoy spending time with aren't the types that ruminate over sports while reading the *Post* at the bar.

Reif's is charming, but has a little too much of that "old man bar" thing going on. Its front room is not so small that you're knocking elbows with the guy sitting next to you, but it's not so big that you can't hear every single word of everyone else's conversations. If you want to know about how NBA rules were changed to counter Wilt Chamberlain's dominance, or the strength of Tim Tebow's NFL prospects, or how Tiger Woods' golf game will be affected by his adultery scandal, you're in luck. If you don't want to know about these things, head for the back. While up front it's stately mahogany and bricks, the rear room is paneled with light-colored wood and features enough accoutrements (pool, darts, Golden Tee, a "Bud Man" cartoon neon sign) to feel like a friend's game room.

When you go back up front you might feel like the jowly guy at the end of the bar is trying to stare you down. But Reif's also offers some nice surprises. When I was there, seven unused credits lingered on the digital jukebox, which I used to play "Bungle in the Jungle." This put me a little more at ease, and seemed to go over well with the dudes. Because, there's hardly a self-respecting man, of any age, who doesn't like Jethro Tull.

Dive Bar Rating

REALLY CHEAP DRINKS

Irish Eyes

Palace Café

Blue & Gold

Nancy Whiskey Pub

Stacks Tavern

Reynold's Café

4241 Broadway (180th Street)

Transit:1 , A ro 181st St (212) 923-8927

"Whatever you do, don't become a bartender," Jim told Matt and me right after a lady with dyed-blonde hair went on a tirade about her baby's daddy, who apparently abandoned her immediately after conception. Reynold's Café's longtime barkeep repeated this maxim a couple more times and then poured himself a drink—Smirnoff and water, no ice. There was Latin music playing and a rambunctious crowd, including two guys who went into the tiny bathroom together, locked the door, and failed to emerge for ten minutes.

An hour earlier, the vibe had been completely different. An entire Joni Mitchell album scrolled through, and Jim told us about the fifty-plus year old Washington Heights tavern's latest technological upgrade. (Also likely its first technological upgrade.) The Guinness "stimulator," he explained, functions as followed: You pour Guinness into a glass and set it in the center of the electronic contraption, which somehow settles the beer and makes it extra smooth.

Reynold's is probably best known for its iconic neon pink sign on the 180th street side, but if anything belongs on the National Register of Historic Places, it's Jim himself. Short, rail-thin, almost-toothless, possessing both sailor-style tattoos on his arm and a near photographic memory for faces, he's been here since long before the neighborhood transitioned from white to brown. (How long exactly? "Mucho, mucho," he says.) The owner has been absent for decades, but he nonetheless calls Jim almost every day to ask him if anyone's in the place. "How many?" he'll inquire. "Count them!"

Jim is a stressed-out guy, but he's a great historian. He explained to us that the mounted animal head near the back of the bar once belonged to a bobcat, and that the mounted critter near the front is a weasel-like species hailing from South America. He then went back to bemoaning his fate, wondering aloud how he had allowed himself to be lured back here out of retirement. He wandered outside for a smoke break every five minutes, each time reminding us before he left, "Whatever you do, don't become a bartender."

Dive Bar Rating

Ruby's Bar & Grill

1213 Boardwalk West, near Stillwell Ave

Transit: D, F, N, Q to Coney Island-Stillwell Ave (718) 372-9079

Ruby's Bar & Grill doesn't normally open for the season until Palm Sunday or Easter. Co-owner Michael Sarrel had jumped the gun the day Anna and I were there, however, to make the most of some unseasonably-warm weather. It was March 20th and the place was chaotic, with just-unpacked beer cases littering the space. Nonetheless, spring fever was in the air, and some saggy women showing shoulder counted down the moments until spring officially began. "3...2...1," they chanted. "It's spring!"

The Coney Island boardwalk is synonymous with the Cyclone roller coaster, the New York Aquarium, heartburn and Ruby's. For more than seventy-five years the spot has epitomized the decadence, lust and inebriation of summer. According to Sarrel, Ruby's once housed a cabaret below the boardwalk, before morphing into a Hebrew National Deli during the depression. His wife's family took it over in the '70s, and nowadays Ruby's is a proudly anachronistic dive that keeps boardwalk creatures full of fried foods and suds.

With walls containing classic Coney Island promotional pictures and black & white prints, Ruby's is a testament to the beach's glory days. But it's sometimes hard to tell if it's coming or going. Rezoning plans threaten to drastically alter the landscape, and there's trash everywhere. Still, tourists continue to flood the area, drawn by the Mets' minor league affiliate, the Brooklyn Cyclones, Nathan's annual hot dog eating competition, nostalgists and the beach itself.

Banners brag that Ruby's was named one of the Travel Channel's "Top 21 Sexiest Beach Bars," which may be true if your idea of sexy is fanny-packing señoras and shirtless old men with tans. Occasionally some bros will come in and ask for Long Island Iced Teas, which Sarrel will grudgingly make, for $12 each. During a difficult 2009, the men's room floor collapsed and sent a guy taking a leak to the hospital, covered in shit. Rumors abounded that the place would be bulldozed. But Ruby's seems to be doing a brisk business again. The ladies showing shoulder had a few rounds out on the plastic chairs on the boardwalk, and a guy with a mullet and a dragon tattoo bought one for his buddy. When a regular plopped down and ordered a beer, Sarrel slid her drink down to her, the bottle sailing smoothly across the frictionless Formica bar.

Dive Bar Rating

Rudy's Bar & Grill

627 9th Ave (44th St & 45th St)   *rudysbarnyc.com*

Transit: A, C, E, 1, 2, 3, S, 7, N, Q, R, W to 42nd St   *(212) 974-9169*

With the exception of the Mars Bar, Rudy's is New York's most famous dive, a beloved Hell's Kitchen institution that opened about five minutes after Prohibition was repealed.

The place is known for its giant pig mascot wearing a valet coat out front, its original wood door with "Rudy" carved in it and free hot dogs, served on napkins. Crowned by antique Tiffany lamps, the booths are all covered in duct tape. The house beers—a red and a terrific blonde -- run you $2.50 for a pint and $7 for a pitcher. A giant tile portrait of a saxophone covers a wall, and the bartenders tend to be pros. One time, the guy serving me wore an undone bow tie and faced a packed house solo. He moved crisply, keeping track of everything and switching quickly between theatre conversations with patrons and Spanish conversations with the help.

There's really not much to dislike about Rudy's, other than the crowding. The back patio "garden"—a stone swath that shows games on a giant, projected TV screen—offers some breathing room when it's open. (In the winter there's a heated tent.) When it's closed, however, there's little space among the young bankers and advertising types who long ago elbowed out the boozy neighborhoodies who used to dominate. Nowadays old-timers who wander in seem out of place, especially after sundown when the post-work crowd settles in. I witnessed a septuagenarian trying in vain to get the attention of another septuagenarian. Though they were only standing five feet away from each other, it was too loud for them to hear one another.

Dive Bar Rating

Smolen Bar & Grill

708 5th Ave (22nd Street)

Transit: R to 25th St

(718) 788-9729

Though its brick façade and bars on the windows are a bit intimidating, Smolen Bar & Grill has a feminine vibe on the inside, which is strange for any dive pub, particularly a Polish one. Especially girly are the decorations—when I was there, fake fall leaves and doll-sized scarecrows—and the television entertainment, in this case a Tori Spelling Christmas special on ABC Family.

The walls are green, and hulking lesbians play Quick Draw in the corner and then duck outside for long smoke breaks. Well-appointed dinner plates with the eagle coat of arms (from the Polish flag) are on display. Zemkoff vodka and quite a few other items in the bar also feature that symbol, which I recognized from my days shopping at Eagle Provisions up the street when I lived nearby. Needless to say, Smolen's has no grill.

A bartender named Pat and her sisters own the place, but running the show the night I was there was a local grandmotherly-type who declined to recommend a Polish beer because she said she didn't drink. However, she did fill me in on the spot's history, positing that Smolen must be at least sixty years old, since she used to walk by it on her way to PS 10 when she was a girl. Back then, she went on, the neighborhood was full of friendly Irish and Italians, and you didn't have to lock your doors or put bars on your pub's windows.

When I was leaving I asked her name, and she said it was Kathy with a "K" and that she went by Kathy Lee. She smiled, and then as I walked out the door one of the lesbians putting out a cigarette told me I was cute. A few friendly types still haunt these parts, it turns out.

Dive Bar Rating

NEW YORK CITY'S BEST DIVE BARS

Sophie's

509 East 5th St (Ave A and Ave B)

Transit: F, M to 2nd Ave   *(212) 228-5680*

"We're All Here Because We're Not All There," reads the sign on the ceiling above the pool table at Sophie's, while a foreboding, blow-up zeppelin hangs over the bar. The drinkery is tucked away in an unmarked storefront on 5th Street, just before that block comes to a screeching halt at Avenue A. It's been at this location for the past twenty years or so—the original opened on 6th Street in 1984—but the paint job on the main wall remains haphazard. It is a mural? Are those white blotches on a burgundy background supposed to be snow falling on Kilimanjaro? More likely the painter just got into the booze before finishing the job. He was probably drinking something from the Bahamas or Bermuda, seeing how liquors of the "islands" were on special when I visited, everything from Kalik Beer to Black Seal Rum.

For the most part, however, this establishment's main influence is from another island, one better known for its tippling. The lads at the end of the bar discuss just what, exactly, it means to be Irish, while the barkeep speaks with just enough of an accent to make you feel faint. (If you're not married, of course.)

With exposed brick, Big Buck Safari and a pool table, Sophie's is similar to most of the other dive bars in the East Village. The clientele, however, happens to be grayer and wiser—or, at the very least drunker—often bearing kids and dogs. One thing to keep in mind: If you're a woman intending using the men's rest room, be sure to have a friend stand look-out, because the door has no lock.

Dive Bar Rating

Stacks Tavern

5723 Broadway (West 234th St and West 236th St)

Transit: 1 to 238th St   *(718) 549-9771*

My friend Rose used to tend bar back in St. Louis, and when we sat down at Stacks Tavern, she asked for some Stoli "with a little dirt." The request threw our ruddy-faced keep for a loop, until she clarified that she meant "olive juice." "Ah," he said, and set about in search of some, to no avail. "No dirt," he said. "We don't have any olives at all, actually. People don't usually come in here and order things like martinis."

Rose ordered Stoli and cranberry instead ($4) to go with my mug of Bud ($1.50), and the bartender brought them out. He seemed impressed to be serving people who would order a martini, and offered us buybacks after our next drinks. After finishing those we were hungry and wanted to order some food. The bartender didn't have any menus, unfortunately, but would do us one better—there were free turkey sandwiches in the corner. Wheat bread and lunch meat with French's mustard, probably from Costco, it turned out. (They were much better than they sound.)

Things are a little different up in the Bronx, particularly on the streets in the mid-230s. Stacks, for example, is a roomy standalone structure, rare for New York pubs. It's got bars on the windows and a gorgeously-tacky narrow red awning that runs the width of the sidewalk. Inside it has a u-shaped bar and a Pacman/Galaga console, but it's the upright version—a surviving '80s relic, likely—rather than the trendy tabletop version. In the winter, the ladies room door remains propped open when not in use because, the bartender explained, the heat doesn't work in there. "The word outhouse," he added, "would certainly apply."

Dive Bar Rating

Station Cafe

39-50 61st St (Roosevelt Avenue)

Transit: 7 to 61st St-Woodside   *Phone disconnected*

WOODSIDE, QUEENS

While the name Station Cafe may conjure up the image of an ornate train station, this Woodside pub is less "Grand Central Station" than "Greyhound bathroom." A sense of deterioration permeates the place, which caters to the grizzled, the Irish and the old. The decorations consist of things like an ancient "No Dancing" poster featuring a pair of tired boxers clutching each other. Expect browning linoleum, duct tape and a side room dedicated to little more than stacks of empties waiting to be recycled, or to decompose or whatever.

As for the booze selection, it's not much, and dusty shelves sit empty behind the bar. This is probably because the staff knows what everyone who walks in is going to want. They're all regulars, and no one's throwing back any aged single malts. Typical answer when the barkeep asks how they're doing? "Good enough."

I read somewhere that all of New York's real dive bars are in Queens, and Station Café certainly brings truth to that statement. Next door to St. Sebastian's Post for Catholic War Veterans, it's also steps away from a bustling transport hub serving the MTA and the Long Island Railroad. Yet somehow it still manages to be the pub that time forgot, or at least the pub whose owners forgot to clean it. You'd probably expect as much from the outside, as Station Cafe's two front display windows are dark and rotting; for some reason, they're backed by wooden slatted blinds and a giant American flag. As you approach you'll think it's closed but have no fear, it's open, despite the fact that the phone is disconnected and the door has no handle. Actually, have a little fear: The Station Cafe, it's clear, caters more to fighters than to dancers.

Dive Bar Rating

The Stoned Crow

85 Washington Place (6th Ave and Washington Square West)
Transit: A, C, E, B, D, F, M to W 4th St; 1 to Christopher St   *(212) 677-4022*

Betty Gordon, owner of The Stoned Crow, presides over the pool table in the back room, lambasting those who interrupt the games by setting their drinks too close to the table. She has a tremendous crop of red hair, and her figure has drawn comparisons to Betty Boop. She has also inspired a series of hand-drawn comics, which are affixed to the wall and usually feature her regulating on some sad sacks who aren't playing by the rules. People also write poems about her. Someone named Sara W. posted this one to Yelp:

> *Lovely Betty, who are you?*
> *You get such pans in these reviews.*
> *Good thing you don't give a flying f**k*
> *'bout all these people slinging muck…*
> *I've never known Betty to block a cue shot,*
> *but if she did, a shot it was not.*
> *So long as you respect the rules,*
> *she'll lower your tab, and that's really cool.*

The ceilings are low at The Stoned Crow and the place is decked out in cobwebs and skeletons. The bathrooms are plastered with old pictures from *Rolling Stone*. (The men's, anyway.) Though the food is expensive—$12 bucks for 10 chicken wings—they've got an actual, fancy pants chef working back there, and the burgers are good.

In any case, most of the action takes place in the back room at this subterranean West Village haunt. The NYU students who rowdy up so many bars in the area tend to stay away, however, perhaps because the music is of the nostalgic, classic rock variety. Truth be told, things get pretty sleepy here when Betty's not around. When she is not here, you kind of wish she would show up and kick somebody's ass.

Dive Bar Rating   ▮▮▮

Subway Inn

143 E 60th St (3rd Avenue & Lexington Ave)

Transit: 4, 5, 6, N, R, W to 59th St-Lex; F to 63rd St   *(212) 223-8929*

Fuck choices. Nobody wants too many choices; they want to be told, more or less, what to do. That's why menus at diners and cheap Chinese restaurants are annoying—preferably, these eateries would do but a few things *well*.

Internet juke boxes similarly offer too many choices. Do we really need access to each Lynyrd Skynrd album? The manual jukeboxes are preferable both because they're cheaper and because they allow watering holes to define their own vibes. Patrons can usually find something they like, and if they can't they probably don't belong there in the first place.

Subway Inn is one bar, however, where an internet jukebox makes sense. The clientele is so varied that no traditional music library could meet its regulars' needs. Located next to Bloomingdales in an area that draws bridge-and-tunnelers, tourists, locals and bums in equal measure, you're likely to see a professor type wearing a bow tie, a trashy dude in a Git-R-Done ball cap and a group of overweight African-American women dancing to Michael Jackson, all in the same visit.

Most famous for its giant red neon sign out front, the seventy-some-year-old Subway Inn seems plucked from a noir film, what with its black-and-white-checkered tile floor, red booths and red lighting. Its many quirks include decorative glass cases housing bags of Snyder's pretzels, Wise chips and plastic Newcastle cups. (The latter are used during weekend rushes, when the bartenders no longer have time to wash the fancy-pants *glass* glasses.) Then there are the Xeroxed "No Smoking" signs on the walls and my personal favorite, a giant, plastic Mich Ultra faux stopwatch that doubles as a barely-functioning clock.

My friend Lavinia calls Subway Inn the perfect rendezvous spot for a sleazy meet-up with a subordinate co-worker. That's an apt description. After all, it affords an anonymity that other spots can't, if only because you blend in no matter what you look like.

Dive Bar Rating

Sunny's Bar

253 Conover St (Beard Street & Reed Street)   *www.sunnysredhook.com*

Transit: Cab it from Smith and 9th Street subway stop (F, G)   *(718) 625-8211*

A grand, bohemian waterfront spot that dates back to the nineteenth century, Sunny's serves as the local pub for the small town that is Red Hook. Its hours are peculiar—Wednesdays, Fridays and Saturday nights only, except for book readings one Sunday afternoon per month—and it's basically off the map, as there are no subways within reasonable walking distance. So, if you don't live nearby you'll have to take a car or (horror of horrors) the bus.

I was there on a cold December night with a pair of folks from Fairbanks, Alaska who said it reminded them of home, both because of its out-of-the-way character and the hearty, full-bearded crowd. Patrons run the gamut from hipsters to longshoreman so thoroughly that it's often impossible to tell an ironic hirsute tippler from a non-ironic one. (The two bartenders that night, one blonde, one brunette, seemed to be engaged in a Rip Van Winkle impersonation contest.) The front room is filled with pale abstract collages, the back room with modern art. At the bluegrass jams and the book readings (hosted by eccentric crime novelist Gabriel Cohen), meanwhile, you'll find some virtuosos and top sellers in the mix. Everything about the place feels like it was meant to be. From the "Avenue P" rest room sign to the toilet seat that won't stay down, to the doors, radiators and fixtures that haven't seen fresh paint in eons, it all meshes seamlessly.

So make the journey to Sunny's, order a vodka gimlet with fresh lime juice upon your arrival, and prepare to be overcome with the desire to discuss some Jack London, or better yet Ernest Hemmingway. Was he gay, or did he just have an emasculating mother? Talk amongst yourselves.

Dive Bar Rating

Three of Cups Lounge

83 1st Avenue, at 5th Street

Transit: F, M to 2nd Ave

(212) 388- 0059

Like Duff's Brooklyn, Three of Cups Lounge is a proud cock rock bar. On any given night you can find rock 'n roll karaoke, DJ Lola X spinning "punk and rock sex grooves," impromptu air guitar competitions, or the Boneyard satellite radio station on the speakers. The oft-scantily clad bartenders bring a bitchin' vibe to the premises as well. A keep who seemed straight out of an L.A. Guns video offered me my choice of "Bad Girl" or "Bad Boy" house shots, which are based in vodka and rum, respectively.

The spot's character couldn't be more different than the downright-respectable Three of Cups restaurant above, which has a wood-burning pizza oven and a menu largely in Italian. (The eatery's co-owner Santo Fazio is known for having helped conceive Two Boots' style of pizza.) But the co-habitation seems an easy one, if only because it's hard to tell from the outside that the two establishments are linked. (Note: the restaurant is known for staying open late, and the drinkery itself doesn't open until mid-evening or so.)

The Lounge's dichromatic insides are almost entirely red and black—except for the leopard-print pole—with dark curtains draping the walls and encased red lights hanging from the ceiling. Tall candles line the tables, and tiny lamps with finely-beaded red covers decorate the walls. A pair of gothic-dressed skeleton dolls sit behind the bar, and the sign for the bathroom promises a "glory hole" inside, although I wasn't lucky enough to encounter that. The rocking out with your cock out, then, must be done figuratively. That's not difficult with anthems from Zebra, Van Hagar and Iron Maiden in regular rotation.

Dive Bar Rating

NEW YORK CITY'S BEST DIVE BARS

Timboo's Bar

477 5th Ave (11th Street)

Transit: F,M,R to 9th St-4th Ave　　　　　　　　　　*(718) 788-9782*

While nearby 5th Avenue pretenders like Buttermilk and Commonwealth grope silently in the dark for that neighborhood-y, unpretentious dive bar vibe, Timboo's Bar hits it on the head without even trying. That's probably because it's been around since before strollers and mustaches dominated these Park Slope streets.

Timboo's has the same sleepy, anachronistic atmosphere as Jackie's 5th Amendment down the way, with only modest updates, including Christmas lights, ads pertaining to NFL games, TVs, pool, darts and live music from time to time. The room is downright purrty, with its polished wood floors and stately ceiling fans. Even the pay phone looks like it's been dusted. The tiles missing from the ceiling in the back room only add to the charm, as does the bizarre wallpaper paying tribute to Manhattan's Empire Diner, complete with '50s-era cars parked out front.

The ironic local gentrifiers are usually absent from the premises. Perhaps they're scared off by all the American flags, but more likely they've been seduced by the ersatz authenticity of Timboo's neighbors. So come to partake in $4.50 pints of Sam Adams and stretch out in the roomy surroundings. But though the men's bathroom is tucked behind the bar and damn hard to find, don't even think about using the better-located women's room, fellas. ("Ladies only!!!" a handwritten sign warns.) Other than that, admire the mammoth, framed encasings featuring Elvis and Beatles paraphernalia, the Travis Tritt platinum record on the wall, and the middle-aged patrons who eat from greasy cardboard baskets of chicken and put Survivor's "The Search Is Over" on the juke. It'll all still be here long after you've left the neighborhood.

Dive Bar Rating

Tip Top Bar & Grill

432 Franklin Ave (Madison Street & Putnam Street)

Transit: C,S to Franklin Ave; G to Classon　　　　*(718) 857-9744*

And on the eighth day, God created the Tip Top Bar & Grill. He covered the doors and windows with iron bars, so no one would mess with paradise. He drenched the inside in glorious Christmas lights of all shapes and colors, including some containing tiny bottles of beer. He then added generous amounts of tinsel. Before taking a break, He created Tip Top's crew:

Corrine, who is in charge of dispensing the food, which is free. Wearing a newsboy cap and glasses that are missing a stem, she serves up Styrofoam plates of wieners, franks, chili, Swedish meatballs, cucumber slices and fish cakes. It's borderline indigestible, but bless Corrine's heart for going to the trouble.

Junior, the owner, who doesn't look a day over seventy. He can be found smoking out front or sitting near the door, carding anyone who looks young, which is pretty much nobody. It's a fair assumption that he was excited about Obama's election, as nearly every inch of Tip Top's wall space is filled with Barack and Michelle pictures—with the queen, with Oprah—and Obama dollar bills.

Linda, the bartender and Junior's daughter. She has long braids and pours a generous drink, so long as you don't order something from a bottle hanging upside down, which are regulated by exact-shot spouts. (Those bottles are even guarded by a counting device to make sure nobody cheats.) Ask to see her personalized, bedazzled "Tip Top" ball cap, which rests on a shelf behind the bar.

Enormous customer, draped in a giant piece of white fabric with a winning smile. She sometimes makes the mistake of eating too much of Corrine's food. At least, one assumes that's what happens, considering her tendency to clutch her side and wreck havoc upon the bathroom.

Sure, He allowed a hurricane to tear apart New Orleans and an earthquake to decimate Haiti, but do not lose faith. He also gave us the Tip Top, the most divinely-inspired dive bar you'll ever get to see.

Dive Bar Rating

The Trash Bar

256 Grand St (Driggs Ave & Roebling St)
Transit: L to Bedford Ave; G,L to Metropolitan Ave-Lorimer St   (718) 599-1000

If The Trash Bar's cluttered main bar is its ego, then its music venue is its id. Though the latter space is quite large, the night I was there it was almost completely devoid of concertgoers. But despite only two paid attendees, the musicians onstage hard-rocked their asses off. This kind of thing apparently happens regularly here; that is, serious axe-grinding for very little glory.

If you're sitting in the bar, the quite-audible live music can leave you anxious and unable to enjoy your tater tots (free with beer). "What if the real party is in the back?" you ask yourself, despite knowing that you've got critical mass here up front with you.

The Trash Bar is positioned near the heart of Williamsburg's hipster vortex, and it's outfitted with décor like minivan seats, Christmas lights and countless band stickers. But the joint attracts a different kind of twenty and thirty-something white person than other area watering holes. These people represent the skuzzier end of hipsterdom; guys with receding hairlines and long, dirty hair; fellas with baggy jeans; dudes who grab their dates' asses at the bar without shame.

Also, there are jokers. After my friend Louis slapped our scratched-up wooden table to make a point, a giant guy walking by (he may have been a bouncer) feigned anger and exclaimed, "Damn! These tables cost money."

"I was finessing it," Louis replied.

The guy laughed. "You looked up like you were scared!"

"I looked up like I was in disbelief."

"My ex-wife had that same look on our honeymoon."

At times like these, it's probably is best to heed your subconscious. Head for the back room, Freud.

Dive Bar Rating

Turkey's Nest Tavern

94 Bedford Ave (11th St and 12th St)
Transit: L to Bedford Ave; G to Nassau Ave   *(718) 384-9774*

It was a cold, wet, mid-February Tuesday night when I journeyed to the Turkey's Nest Tavern. A few snowflakes fell, continuing the month's onslaught. It was a miserable night, suddenly made brighter by a parade moving down Bedford Avenue, seemingly out of nowhere. "It's the first annual Brooklyn Mardi Gras parade," enthused a man with a microphone atop a float. "Get excited!" The float was done up in pastel crepe paper and had an actual police escort. The marchers were not many, but they were dressed in masks, dresses, heels and other New Orleans-inspired accoutrements, and tossed plastic necklaces to folks watching from the sidewalk. The most enthusiastic responses came from smokers congregating outside of Turkey's Nest, one who promised he would show his "wee wee" in exchange for some beads. The event was sponsored by *L Magazine*, but had a spontaneous feel to it, and its participants were of the same relative demographic of those at the Turkey's Nest.

Imbibers at this Bedford hipster dive don't need an excuse as formal as Mardi Gras to get lively, however, and can be found making merry inside its wood-paneled walls most any time. Late night on the weekends it's often completely packed, which can make the line for the men's room ("Turkey's") and the women's room ("Turkette's") quite unbearable.

Absinthe margaritas are on offer for seven dollars, but the spot is best known for four dollar Styrofoam quarts of Bud and Coors Light and four buck plastic pints of their home-brew, called Turkey Beer. The only thing is, they don't actually brew said beer themselves, and it changes according to what brand of keg was on sale that week. "So, what I am drinking?" I inquired of the chillaxed bartendress, clad in a "Rocks Off" sweatshirt. "I honestly have no idea," she replied.

Dive Bar Rating ▲▲▲▲

Vazac's Horseshoe Bar / 7B

108 Avenue B (Corner of Avenue B and 7th St)
Transit: F, V to 2nd Ave   *(212) 473-8840*

Vazac's Horseshoe Bar / 7B is a carnival funhouse, a labyrinth, an arcade. Large by East Village standards, the plethora of space permits multiple gaming options. Besides Big Buck Hunter, Golden Tee and CSI pinball, there's a console offering electronic bean bag toss and lawn darts. Wait, what?

Named both for the depression-era catering hall it replaced (Vazac's) and the corner on which it sits (Avenue B and 7th Street), the Horseshoe Bar has supposedly played host to the filming of movies like The Godfather Part II, Cocktail and Serpico. But its vibe doesn't really fit with those flicks, as it's usually filled by an unlikely mix of fat old guys, cool kids, sports fans and workaday rabble rousers.

But don't get me wrong. Anyone can feel comfortable here, what with its bevy of flat screens showing games, dozens of beers on tap and drink deals. (A double-decker can of Labatt Blue is five bucks.) Perhaps its best feature is its punk-and-metal-oriented jukebox, which has Slayer, Helmet, Murder City Devils, New York Dolls and the Supersuckers, not to mention the soundtracks to both Dead Presidents and Repo Man. The horseshoe-shaped bar at the room's center is buttressed by roman-style columns, which are flanked by ramshackle booths and odd nooks and crannies. A corner with nothing but a stool and a video poker machine is one of many spots to semi-discretely make out, if you're into that sort of thing. Because of the tavern's confusing layout, people often need two passes to locate the men's room—where they might encounter, as I did, someone puking their guts out. Another architectural quirk is the staircase to nowhere. Crammed with overturned chairs, trash bags and old neon beer signs, it twists a few times before arriving directly at the ceiling.

Time breaks down at Vazac's. The memorabilia on the walls is both retro—like the framed newspaper announcing "Lindbergh over France!"—and faux retro, like the "Kamel" cigarettes Vargas girl ads. Decades-old band stickers line the walls, and the bathroom is coated in many coats of sloppy gray paint. It's all a glorious, sprawling mess.

Dive Bar Rating

WCOU Radio (Tile Bar)

115 First Ave (7th Street)
Transit: 6 to Astor Place; L to 1st Ave   *(212) 254-4317*

Unless you're the type to be razzle-dazzled by a white-and-black checkerboard floor and some colored tiles, you'll find WCOU Radio a simple, no frills spot. The WCOU neon clock, Jim Jarmusch movie posters and turn-of-the-century downtown New York pictures are just about the only things on the walls.

It's a great bar to have in your back pocket when you're in the East Village. Drinks aren't expensive by local standards, and like its sister bars WXOU Radio in the West Village and The Magician on the Lower East Side, it isn't crowded when you think it should be crowded. You'll be able to snag a table or a seat at the bar even during prime drinking hours. Hopefully you've brought along someone interesting to talk to, however, because the crowd tends toward milquetoast grad student types. Try as you might, you won't be able to spot a single person who is not a Caucasian between the ages of 26 and 34. Most of them have messy hair; not fashionably messy or greasy, just "I'm not going to let the fascist beauty industry bully me into combing my hair" messy. There's the occasional woman in a ponytail and plenty of guys with facial hair—not beards or 'staches, though, just stubble, and not "sexy" stubble, just "haven't shaved" stubble. But it's easy to tune these folks out, as the lighting is just dim enough and it's not as loud as you'd expect such a small room to be. The jukebox boasts sufficient out-of-the-box choices to satisfy—Dwight Yoakam, say, to counterbalance the requisite Sam Cooke and Patsy Cline

When you're at the Tile Bar, it's easy to forget you're in a trendy Manhattan neighborhood. Everybody's talking about centrifuges and evolutionary biology and third wave feminism, for one thing, and they're dressed like schlubs. But hey, if they stay out of your way, then *prost* to them.

Dive Bar Rating

Welcome to the Johnson's

123 Rivington St (Essex St & Norfolk St)

Transit: F, J, M, Z to Delancey-Essex   *(212) 420-9911*

Welcome to the Johnson's resembles the den of a Midwestern house, circa 1975, down to the wood-paneled wall featuring portraits of family members wearing bowl cuts. One couch is covered in plastic, while the other is too grimy to sit on. Also: fake ferns, marbled glass, a plastic Santa wearing a trucker cap, random baseball trophies, and cubby hole shelves. You get the idea. The whole thing feels very calculated until you get to the bathrooms, which are filled with standing water.

Normally, old movies play on the TV (and sometimes porn), but when I was there the library of videocassettes was gone and the TV was blasting static. The bartender explained that the set no longer got reception because of the digital switchover, but that didn't make any sense because the switchover was still months away. "Now it's just like we're showing Poltergeist all the time," she added chirpily.

You're unlikely to find a cheaper drink on the Lower East Side than the $1.75 happy hour PBRs they keep in a box full of ice. And so long as you fit their demographic—Generation Y, Obama-voting, Twitter-using—you will likely enjoy your time at Welcome to the Johnson's. But if you don't fit the demo, or you just don't feel like hanging out in a bar where people hold book club meetings, it might not be your kind of place.

Hipsters are often accused of "fetishizing the authentic," which sounds like a dirty thing to do. But when you're fetishizing your own, boring childhood—and even going to great lengths to recreate it—it doesn't seem as sleazy. Rather, it's comforting. If you were born in the Midwest during the Carter years like I was, Welcome to the Johnson's might even feel like home

Dive Bar Rating

Winnie's Bar and Restaurant

104 Bayard St (Baxter Street and Mulberry St)
Transit: J, M, Z, N, Q, R, W, 6 to Canal St   *(212) 732-2384*

A certified Chinatown institution, Winnie's Bar and Restaurant has no shame in its game. Just like Katz's Deli knows tourists will pay sixteen dollars or whatever for one of their pastrami sandwiches, Winnie's knows that its nine buck shots of mid-shelf whiskey will be gladly thrown back by slumming Park Slope web consultants.

Famous for being grimy, Winnie's is perched on the street level but feels underground, what with the low light, low ceiling and lack of street noise. Like many dives it features red vinyl booths and cardboard boxes of beer ringing the premises, but its massive, anachronistic karaoke system is its main claim to fame. A giant-screen TV is surrounded by ancient AV equipment and songbooks. The system operates via laser discs, which offer both lyrics and soap opera-style vignettes. Couples walk down beaches, stare into each others' eyes or admire sailboats while a sixty-year-old man performs an eastern-accented version of Barbra Streisand's "The Way We Were." Winnie's charges a dollar for karaoke, and the drinks and food are even more of a rip-off. The menu features but two items, spring rolls and dumplings, each $8 and slightly less delicious than those you'd find at the back of your bodega's freezer.

Ultimately, the place gets by on chutzpah alone. As Anna put it, it's the kind of joint you go after you're already drunk. In that frame of reference it would probably seem pretty exotic, a whimsical outpost that time has forgotten, full of thin-mustached locals and cute Chinese bartenders. So what if it's actually a lean, mean, capitalist machine?

Dive Bar Rating

JERSEY CITY AND HOBOKEN DIVES

Having lived in Hoboken for a couple of years, I'm something of a New Jersey apologist. But though Hoboken and Jersey City are technically part of that dreaded, parasite state, they're effectively outer boroughs of New York City. They've got the same density, same architecture, and in fact harbor some of the diviest bars in the metro area. The best part is that most of them are a quick ride away from Manhattan on the PATH train.

Burke's Bar & Discount Liquors
596 Grove Street, Jersey City
(201) 656-4611
Transit: Pavonia/Newport (PATH)

Located at the doorstep of the Holland Tunnel, Burke's Bar looks like a regular old seedy liquor store from the outside. Upon entry, however, you'll notice, voila! bar stools, making for the strangest little den of commerce you'll ever encounter. The clientele is mainly culled from the nearby Salvation Army mission, and the drinks aren't as cheap as they probably should be. But, hey, if it's not your scene, you can always just grab a case to go.

DC's Tavern
505 8th Street, Hoboken
(201) 792-5550
Transit: Hoboken (PATH), and then a hike

The door to DC's Tavern looks like the door to somebody's house, and opens outward. When you walk in everyone stares at you, because you've basically entered their living room. But despite the limited elbow room, DC's host concerts on occasion, not to mention record swaps and CD release parties from groups like Turbonegro. "Whoever can't get in, doesn't fit in," the bartender explained to me.

Golden Cicada Tavern
195 Grand Street, Jersey City
(201) 432-0048
Transit: Grove St (PATH)

In Manhattan, a double shot of Dewar's will cost you about $15. At Golden Cicada Tavern, a triple shot cost me that much, and they also threw in beers for Anna and my friends Will and Gina. This brick hut on the corner of Grand and Marin is a Jersey City institution, a bit grimy but quite serviceable. The food is solid—a plate of pork chops and fries will set you back about seven bucks—but don't peek into the kitchen or you might lose your appetite.

Lucky 7
322 2nd Street, Jersey City
(201) 418-8585
Transit: Grove St (PATH)

A tremendously friendly neighborhood dive in Jersey City that sponsors the local roller derby team, Bridge & Pummel. Those smashing ladies and the pictures on the walls show a typical cross-section of the type of Lucky 7 types; hipsters, yes, but a bit more grizzled and hard-drinking than your typical Williamsburger. And speaking of burgers, they are worth sampling here. Try the Don Ho—with pineapple, Canadian bacon, and sautéed onions—or, even better, the Jersey, with roasted red peppers, jalapenos, chipotle mayo and pepper jack cheese.

Lucky 7

Mario's Bar
301 Park Street, Hoboken
(201) 659-9461
Transit: Hoboken (PATH)

Perhaps the most classic dive bar in the greater New York area, Mario's Bar in Hoboken is just about perfect. You'll think it's closed when you get there, and it's as quiet and dark as a tomb inside. The barkeep is a crotchety, hilarious, septuagenarian Czech, the wood-paneled bathrooms reek of urine, and there's not much selection. Behind the bar sit dozens of jugs of a syrupy California wine called Paul Masson.

Ringside Lounge
475 Tonnele Avenue, Jersey City
(201) 963-1777
Transit: You're gonna have to drive

The unofficial capital of Jersey City's underworld, it's got a bad reputation for ladies of the night, as well as dudes bearing synthetic solutions to your very-real problems. If that doesn't put you off, this boxing-themed establishment has serviceable-ish food, cheap drinks and sports action. That said, the patrons are more interesting than what's on the television.

Rolon's Bar Inc.
242 Bay Street, Jersey City
(201) 333-9866
Transit: Grove St (PATH)

No I don't have any idea why a Jersey City dive with a 360-degree swiveling register is called "Inc," but Rolon's Bar Inc. is a gem. Catering to a primarily Latin American clientele, Rolon's serves well drinks in wine glasses, and the cumbia is always blasting. There's no toilet in the men's room, only a urinal. The square-shaped bar wraps all the way around the place, and if you want citrus for your Corona, the cute-beyond-belief old man bartender will hand you a Tupperware container containing pre-cut limas.

Wilton House
58 Newark Street, Hoboken
(201) 656-9635
Transit: Hoboken (PATH)

With its tremendous quantity of bars per capita, the Mile Square City has a reputation as a drinker's haven, but of the worst kind. Immediately after getting off the PATH train, Hoboken visitors are besieged by frat boys, drunken football fans and guidos lining up at overpriced bars and clubs. But a couple blocks further into town you'll find Wilton House, a deliciously-bare bones dive that lacks bells, whistles or assholes. Composed mainly of a long bar facing a mirror with the bar's name and a pair of horsey heads, Wilton House is cheap and tidy. The coasters say, "We're Glad You're Here," and you're just glad you're not rubbing elbows with 'roided-up Jets fans.